# BIG, BOLD

&

*Beautiful*

OWNING THE WOMAN GOD MADE YOU TO BE

# BIG, BOLD & Beautiful

## KIERRA SHEARD-KELLY

ZONDERVAN

*Big, Bold, and Beautiful*
Copyright © 2021 by Kierra Sheard

Requests for information should be addressed to:
Zondervan, 3900 Sparks Dr. SE, Grand Rapids, Michigan 49546

Library of Congress Cataloging-in-Publication Data

Names: Sheard, Kierra Kiki, author.
Title: Big, bold, and beautiful: owning the woman God made you to be / Kierra Sheard.
Description: Hardcover. | Grand Rapids, Michigan : Zondervan, [2021] | Audience: Ages
    16-19 | Audience: Grades 10-12 | Summary: "In this immersive and inspirational
    book for teens, Grammy Award-nominated singer Kierra Sheard shares her hard-won
    advice on body positivity, spiritual self-care, goal setting, finding your joy, and living
    boldly in faith, empowering you to grab the life you're meant to lead. Every one of us
    was born to make a difference. But do you sometimes feel overwhelmed by the things
    the world prioritizes, thinking you don't match up or you don't fit into the mold? Or
    do you wish you had a more supportive family, or positive role models, or access to the
    things you need emotionally and spiritually to keep going? Kierra Sheard sees you and
    will teach you how to: *Identify your goals, talents, and gifts so you can survive and
    thrive *Deal with societal expectations and focus on what really matters *Truly love
    yourself and find out who you really are as an individual *Live your faith loud and
    proud"— Provided by publisher.
Identifiers: LCCN 2020040715 (print) | LCCN 2020040716 (ebook) | ISBN 9780310770800
    (Hardcover) | ISBN 9780310770817 (Ebook) | ISBN 9780310770824 (Audio download)
Subjects: LCSH: Self-actualization (Psychology) in women—Juvenile literature. |
    Christian women—Religious life—Juvenile literature. | Well-being—Religious
    aspects—Juvenile literature. | Women—Conduct of life—Juvenile literature.
Classification: LCC BF637.S4 S5165 2021 (print) | LCC BF637.S4 (ebook) |
    DDC 158.1—dc23
LC record available at https://lccn.loc.gov/2020040715
LC ebook record available at https://lccn.loc.gov/2020040716

*Cover Design: Cindy Davis*
*Cover Photography: Mel B. Elder Jr.*
*Interior Design: Denise Froelich*

*Printed in Canada*

21  22  23  24  25  /  TC  /  10  9  8  7  6  5  4  3  2

*I dedicate this book to my nanna. She left too soon. I began reading more books because of the first book she gave me, which changed my life. I hope that this book does the same for someone as the book Nanna gave me.*

*I also dedicate this to my Popoo, who has taught me some of my greatest life lessons, which I share throughout this book.*

*In addition, I dedicate this to my amazing husband, Jordan Kelly. I honor you and the change that you've brought to my life. I also dedicate this to my wonderful parents who are responsible for the woman I am today; my brother, J. Drew, who is my first best friend; my family, friends, and KiChain, who have been so supportive of me and all that I do. I wouldn't have the wisdom to share if it weren't for you. I love you.*

# Contents

Chapter 1    Self-Care and Squad Goals . . . . . . . . . . . . . . . . . . . 1

Chapter 2    Finding Your Tribe. . . . . . . . . . . . . . . . . . . . . . . . . . 5

Chapter 3    If They Can't Make the Journey,
You May Have to Leave Them Behind . . . . . . . . . 10

Chapter 4    Make the Most of It . . . . . . . . . . . . . . . . . . . . . . . 15

Chapter 5    Big and Bold. . . . . . . . . . . . . . . . . . . . . . . . . . . . 20

Chapter 6    Don't Rush Your Process . . . . . . . . . . . . . . . . . . . 26

Chapter 7    The Silver Spoon . . . . . . . . . . . . . . . . . . . . . . . . 34

*Blessings on Blessings* . . . . . . . . . . . . . . . . . . . 40

Chapter 8    Stop Comparing Yourself . . . . . . . . . . . . . . . . . . 41

Chapter 9    God as My Agent . . . . . . . . . . . . . . . . . . . . . . . . 45

Chapter 10    Pick Up the Pieces and Grab the Glue . . . . . . . . . 50

Chapter 11    Doing It God's Way . . . . . . . . . . . . . . . . . . . . . . . 55

Chapter 12    Successfully Single . . . . . . . . . . . . . . . . . . . . . . . 60

Chapter 13    Past Mistakes Don't Determine Your Future . . . . . 66

Chapter 14    Stop Looking at the Other Woman
(Because You've Got the Juice) . . . . . . . . . . . . . . 73

Chapter 15    Never Mind. I'm Redefining It! . . . . . . . . . . . . . . . 78

Chapter 16    Chill Out!. . . . . . . . . . . . . . . . . . . . . . . . . . . . . . . 83

*Mind, Body, and Spirit* . . . . . . . . . . . . . . . . . . . 88

Chapter 17    A Good Man . . . . . . . . . . . . . . . . . . . . . . . . . . . . 90

Chapter 18    Gimme My Money. . . . . . . . . . . . . . . . . . . . . . . . 96

Chapter 19    Splurge . . . a Little. . . . . . . . . . . . . . . . . . . . . . . 101

*Six Ways to Secure the Bag* . . . . . . . . . . . . . . . . . 105

Chapter 20   I'm Not a Businessman, I'm a BUSINESS, Man!. . 109
Chapter 21   Cheat Days . . . . . . . . . . . . . . . . . . . . . . . . . . . . 115

*Forget the Dumb Stuff* . . . . . . . . . . . . . . . . . . . . 119

Chapter 22   Save Something for Yourself . . . . . . . . . . . . . . . 121
Chapter 23   Kill the Dragon . . . . . . . . . . . . . . . . . . . . . . . . 125
Chapter 24   Hearing God's Voice . . . . . . . . . . . . . . . . . . . . 131
Chapter 25   I'm Supposed to Be Here . . . . . . . . . . . . . . . . . 135
Chapter 26   Say Less. . . . . . . . . . . . . . . . . . . . . . . . . . . . . 140

*Remind Yourself* . . . . . . . . . . . . . . . . . . . . . . . . 145

Chapter 27   The Drains and the Fountains . . . . . . . . . . . . . 147
Chapter 28   Closure. . . . . . . . . . . . . . . . . . . . . . . . . . . . . . 151
Chapter 29   People Problems . . . . . . . . . . . . . . . . . . . . . . 157

*Lower Your Expectations* . . . . . . . . . . . . . . . . . . 164

Chapter 30   Putting Down the Weight of Guilt and
             Picking Up the Weight of Glory. . . . . . . . . . . . . 166
Chapter 31   Fearless and Unbothered. . . . . . . . . . . . . . . . . 171
Conclusion   Owning It All. . . . . . . . . . . . . . . . . . . . . . . . . . 175

*Acknowledgments* . . . . . . . . . . . . . . . . . . . . . . . 179
*Connect with Kierra* . . . . . . . . . . . . . . . . . . . . . . 181
*About the author.* . . . . . . . . . . . . . . . . . . . . . . . . 183

# CHAPTER 1

# Self-Care and Squad Goals

I learned at an early age that you need to protect yourself and what you feel the most passionate about in order to succeed. And for my mommy and nanna, when holiday meals rolled around, what they were most protective of was their kitchen and their food.

They couldn't stand for too many people to be in the kitchen, because it meant they couldn't be the most productive or make their best food. Sometimes people would just take up space, and others weren't there to help cook or even keep the space tidy and help serve the meals being made—those people got the boot before long. Children were never allowed because they weren't mature and seasoned enough to handle what was around them; they could hurt themselves in a slip, cut themselves, break something important like the fine china, or accidentally cause someone else to make a mistake. And even once I was old enough, my mother and nanna didn't always like me in the kitchen because, while I would help, I would also have a personal taste fest along the way. Before you knew it, some of the food would be missing and my kitchen time came to an end.

They were also a bit protective of their recipes, only giving a hint of the secrets behind them to keep each a family tradition. Unless you were going to carry on their traditions, you had no business learning their secrets. That's because when you're building a legacy and working to leave your mark in the world, not everyone can be a part of that.

Now I see that those same rules apply to everyday life, including mental health and building legacies. You should be very protective with your recipes and space—whether it's a passion for making music or ideas you have for new products, or even the time you need to focus on a goal you want to achieve. So don't feel the need to keep people around if they're getting in the way of your success or your purpose. Some hard decisions will need to be made to maintain and build your legacy. And you'll discover some of the people around you are real family who are worthy of what you have to offer, and some are guests just there for the meal.

To determine which relationships are for a lifetime, and which ones have an expiration date, ask yourself, "Who's my 'family'?" Remove the people who are just taking up space, remove those with childlike tendencies and mentalities. Make sure they are mature enough to handle your greatness and where you're going. You'll need some *wise* counsel from time to time. Will they know what to say? Then protect your recipes. Sometimes to build big empires, it doesn't take the amount of people we think. Do the people helping you build only make life about what they want, or is it about everyone winning together?

Are the people in your circle keeping you centered and sane? Chatting about your "wins" too often may offend some who are used to losing, so make sure your squad will genuinely enjoy your wins and not be intimidated by what God is doing in your life. Especially because when your squad is not happy and putting off a negative vibe, it may cause you to carry the weight of guilt and later feel defeat.

Finally, what is the legacy you're trying to build? What part of your life needs more of your attention to accomplish your goals? Maybe it's a focus on the first steps you need to take toward your dream, growing your relationships with friends and family so you have the support, prioritizing your goals—or even just spending more time focusing on yourself and your needs. Self-care is necessary. Just like too many people in the kitchen makes preparing meals difficult, taking on too much at one time can sometimes lead you to lose focus on what you want to create. And just because things aren't coming out the way you want them to right now doesn't mean they won't improve down the line. It's all about the season and making sure you have the right plan in place. And recognizing the God-given makeup of what you have inside and what the current season requires of you to accomplish.

_____**prayer**

*Lord, I thank you for trusting me with a dream and vision. Thank you for life. Father, I ask that you protect me from people who aren't supposed to be in my kitchen while cooking up what you've assigned to me. Give me the grace to accept who's supposed to be in my space, but give me the strength to kindly release people who aren't sent by you. Sharpen my discernment and line of communication with you, so that I can identify who's an answer and who's a trap. Help me to identify counterfeits, so that I'm saying yes to the right people and yes to the right doors. Continue to show me how to grow in you and trust in you, whether it be through more supportive relationships, prayer, or reading more to build myself for what you have planned for me. In Jesus's name, I pray. Amen.*

_____**scriptures to consider**

But the Lord said to Gideon, "There are still too many men. Take them down to the water, and I will thin them out for you there. If I say, 'This one shall go with you,' he shall go; but if I say, 'This one shall not go with you,' he shall not go. . . . The Lord said to Gideon, "With the three hundred men that lapped I will save you and give the Midianites into your hands. Let all the others go home."

**JUDGES 7:4, 7**

# CHAPTER 2

# Finding Your Tribe

**K**nowing who to hold tight to and who to cut loose can sometimes be hard—something I've learned firsthand many times in my life.

One of the greatest lessons in knowing who I needed to keep was with my best friend, Courtney, who is able to speak life into me right when I need it. In one instance, I remember calling her immediately following an awful argument with a guy I had dated for a long time. I had asked him to leave, and as I drove him home, we exchanged harsh words laced with hard-to-accept truths. The cutting blow came when he called me out of my name, and our verbal fighting escalated quickly after that. At the time I was truly a sight to see—I had on a gown and a head wrap, and my emotions were right on the surface. Afterward, I called Court yelling and crying, saying, "I can't believe he did this." She stayed calm, asked where I was, and made sure I was safe. And as I explained what happened, she just listened. She didn't interrupt me. While I told her he'd called me out of my name, did this and that and that, she didn't judge me. Mind you, I'd called Court with the same stories about this relationship many, many times. So she totally could have said, "But we all told you to let that go." She didn't do that. In that moment, she saw her friend was depleted, in disbelief, and broken.

Once she had a chance to speak, she immediately empowered me with healing words. Court reminded me of what I am and said, "What you heard is what you're not!" It was like she was attempting to erase the words that had been thrown at me and began rebuilding my mental space, where I house who I am. Her anger over my feeling put down and broken came through the phone, and she said, "I hope you never go back again." She was just as disgusted as I was, and she kept saying, "He may be for somebody, but he certainly isn't for you." Later, when I mentioned other challenges to Court, she gave me truth and warned me I needed to get out. Somehow, she presented the truth with kindness. The other blessing in this sister-bond was that my friend wasn't afraid to tell me the truth. While I felt worthless, she helped me remember my worth with restorative words. To have friends who aren't insensitive to your hurt is so necessary. I remember saying to Court, "I know you're tired of hearing the same story." She said, "I'm not. This is what we do. We are here for each other to hear the same stories until we figure it out together." For her, my "you" problems were "we" problems she was happy to take on.

Who can you go to when it all becomes too much? Think back to moments when someone really supported you while you were in a bad place—mentally, emotionally, or even financially. Or look on your phone to see the contacts you go back to over and over because they lift you back up when things knock you down. These are the people God put in your life because he knew you would need them when you hit this place in your journey. In a tribe, people usually share social, economic, and religious similarities and we come through strong for one another. Imagine having a tribe or a village of people (your closest, most trusted circle) who are spiritually sound and able to see the spirit and motive behind the life challenges and new people who come into your life. In that same tribe, imagine having a safe haven that makes you feel priceless when being elsewhere makes you feel worthless. This tribe reminds you of your value, which keeps you on course toward your life's purpose. Because when we are off course and unsure of who we are, we lose confidence in the Lord and in ourselves. As a result, we allow anyone and anything to come into our lives, claiming things for themselves or treating our lives as rental spaces.

Also think about who could become a go-to over time. Maybe you've felt the friend you went to in the past isn't in a place she can support you the way you need anymore. We all change at some point. And at different levels of your life, you might meet new people and need new resources. Is there someone you've just met who has the potential to become your ride or die when it comes to handling relationships, or just getting your business in order? Foster those connections, and respond in the same kindness they show you.

_____**prayer**

*Father, I thank you for placing people in my life to uphold and encourage me. Show me the friends and family in my life who I can go to, who will support me and speak your words to me when things are hard and I feel at the end of my rope. And God, please place new people in my life so I have the support I need in the days and times to come as well. I thank you for the blessings you have given me and the past you have helped me to overcome. Remind me that you are my ultimate support and go-to no matter what circumstances I find myself in. Help me to remember that you often love on me through people, but that the enemy uses people to complete his assignment as well. So, as I understand the importance of who I have in my life, please increase my level of discernment so that I say yes to the right people. Please don't allow me to be blind or in darkness. Help me to be confidently selective with my choices in friends so that I am not unknowingly adding to my spiritual warfare. Surround me with truth and love. Remove yes men and give me people who are concerned with my spirit and destiny. In Jesus's name, amen.*

_____scriptures to consider

A friend loves at all times, and a brother is born for a time of adversity.

PROVERBS 17:17

Perfume and incense bring joy to the heart, and the pleasantness of a friend springs from their heartfelt advice.

PROVERBS 27:9

# CHAPTER 3

# If They Can't Make the Journey, You May Have to Leave Them Behind

Stop expecting commitment from people who aren't committed to themselves.

I know now I have to make the most of my life, with who I have and what I have. But in the beginning stages of my business, Eleven60, I was focused on building a team because we were growing. There were some around me who were down for the grind and there were some who weren't. I started taking the "uncommitted" people's behavior personally. However, I eventually started considering everything about them, and myself, to better understand why those people just wouldn't stick. And when I began paying attention to the people I had around, and their ages, there were a few common denominators. Some were still trying to figure out life at the same time I was asking them to come on board with a certain kind of security already within themselves in order to journey with me. And while I knew what my business would turn out to be in the long term, others on my team weren't as turned on to that future; or in some cases, they simply didn't believe in it.

But as I traveled this journey, it was hard to stop seeing everything that was happening with these people as a reflection on *me*. I tried to show interest in their personal lives, always making sure I wasn't a great businesswoman who then had absolutely no regard for those on her team. I gave more than seemed necessary to build relationships, but when things needed to be done right and in order, my feedback wasn't received well because my teammates and I were so close in age; they dismissed me. I also remember people coming onto the team wanting to be there, but only halfway. It was kind of frustrating when they would mention other companies as more of a priority than mine. And even when I got what I could out of them, very often the Lord wouldn't let me to get too comfortable with how things were going, because it began to feel like my business had a revolving door; people would leave after a short time, or I would end up having to release them if I felt they were only there to have fun.

For a long time I picked at myself about why people wouldn't stick, and I began reflecting. People gravitated toward the glamorous parts of the work, but when it was time to load trailers for pop-up shops, they weren't so down for the cause. They wanted the flights to different cities but didn't want to learn the systems that were in place for the integrity of the business and brand. Or it could've simply been that people weren't as down to take risks like I was. I remember my uncle Ethan telling me to "stop expecting people to think like you." I started questioning myself and asking what I needed to do better. I thought more about the people who left than the people who stayed.

And during this entire process, here's the biggest thing I learned about myself: I *did* expect people to think like me. And I was wrong. A lot of that mindset came from the fact I had been trained to work hard, appreciate, and Dream Big at a young age. So while the people on my team and I were similar in age, my goals were more about building legacy than going out to get a drink. We were simply in different places, and I couldn't let those people remain my focus. Instead, I needed to focus on people who had the same drive and could bring a perspective I didn't have that would help my business thrive.

And I found that key person. My friend Shamika quit her job and joined me around the time everyone was coming and going. She and I had our differences, but we stuck together through it. We learned what would work and what wouldn't. We matched when it came to being in the grind, making sacrifices, and remaining students who learned from each other and others. We were open to correction. We worked on ourselves so we were able to see the challenges that could be overcome. We made adjustments and realized we could do what everyone else had thought was hard, all by ourselves. Hence, we sat down, put our minds together, and were able to organize things a bit better so everything worked smoother when working with new people and adjusting to their perspectives. We've now had an array of TV shows, artist contracts, radio deals, major establishments, and so much more come across our desk. Opportunities we previously couldn't even imagine. God blessed us to keep moving with what we had and without missing what we left behind. And throughout this process, my friend and I became renaissance women, and Shamika is now building her business while we still work together.

Maybe people have left you or let you down. Sometimes feeling alone is a part of the process, but God will send you a "Shamika." Someone who believes in you and who is down for it all. In the meantime, hold tight to what you know is true and stay bold in spirit. Sometimes there are people we have said yes to that the Lord is driving out of our lives. It may feel like rejection when it could simply be us not having consulted with God about their presence in our circle, so he finds a way to remove them for us.

_____prayer

*Father, I thank you for the dream you've put inside of me. I ask that you settle my spirit and help me live with contentment in my heart. I ask that you allow me to think big and own the decisions so I actually do what you've set before me. I pray you surround*

13

*me with people who will come alongside to help me make the most of every opportunity. I ask you give me the strength, and the peace, to release relationships that are no longer of service to me, or to my assignment on earth. Father, I ask that I be more concerned with your will, so that I am not surprised when things don't go my way. I also ask that you give me the confidence in you so that people, or their opinions, don't cause me to second guess the vision, gift, or idea you've put inside of me. Amen.*

_____scriptures to consider

They confronted me in the day of my disaster,
but the Lord was my support.

**PSALM 18:18**

God is within her, she will not fall; God will
help her at break of day.

**PSALM 46:5**

# CHAPTER 4

# Make the Most of It

Don't get me wrong, I work hard, and building the life you dream of takes a lot of work. Success isn't for slackers. But at the same time, if all you do is work and focus on one area of your life, you will miss the opportunities around you. Not to mention leave yourself so empty, you won't have the strength to push toward the big things, weakening your potential as you burn yourself out. You, and your life, are about more than the grind.

While we were building our company, my friend Shamika and I made the decision to make the most of every business trip, and we had opportunities to travel in and out of the country on numerous occasions. My homegirl and I focus on the work we need to do, but we have also seen the greatest shopping malls, experienced some of the greatest amusement parks, traveled first class, dined at some of the world's greatest restaurants, and so much more. After a while, the days of hard work didn't feel like "work" but a life journey of fun, purpose, and money. Ha!

But this only began when we decided to start making the most of it all. We turned our business trips into "Live your life" trips. We'd go in a day early or stay a day longer to enjoy the city. And over time we learned that when there were days where we needed to do some problem solving for the business, we dressed for the occasion and we got the job done.

I remember having a business trip in West Africa, and I had been wanting to go to South Africa for so long. Shamika and I had already begun making it a habit to "make the most of it," and I immediately said, "South Africa! Let's add it. It would be cheaper because it's closer." We began exploring the cost of flights from South Africa to West Africa, and it looked doable. So what did I do? I added to the trip. I made sure the extra stops paid for themselves and that I wasn't over budget and could still do first class. Nothin' against coach, but honey, these hips are too wide to sit that long in those seats! And at that point, I had also decided I would live it up, because this was a once-in-a-lifetime chance.

In the end, Shamika came to West Africa, and we had so much fun, but she couldn't make the South Africa trip. Usually, I would put things to a halt and wait for others to "live," but I made up my mind that I would start doing things on my own. I had my trip booked and headed off by myself.

(However, my loved ones didn't want me to go *completely* alone, so a friend who is like a big brother, Dante, popped in on me.) I took myself to Cape Town and Johannesburg. I gave myself a mini world tour in my other home. I also had in mind to go and look at their fashion. I planned to see what design concepts I could create for my fashion line while globalizing my mind and ways of thinking overall. And I had a great experience with God. Walked with the cheetah. Sat with the lion cubs. Learned more about where I'm from and more. Later, Shamika and I received another offer from Africa. We then said, "DUBAI!" These two big girls were making the most of it! It was then Korea to Thailand. New York to D.C., and so many other opportunities. We were dreaming and living big and were OWNING IT!

Maybe your "making the most of it" is different from mine, but in what ways can you stretch yourself? Is it a change of scenery, meeting new friends, adjusting the way you spend your time or money? What will you do with your downtime? Once you get to the place you'd like to be, will you have enough discipline to *have* downtime? Self-care is so necessary. Reflect mentally. Don't wait on anyone to do the things you've been dreaming of doing. Of course, be safe, but go for it! And if you're on the fence, consult with friends to ensure you aren't being irrational and instead see the abundance of life God has promised us. For instance, I used to wait to do certain things with a boyfriend, husband, or friend because it seemed like the right thing to do, or because I thought the experience would be most enjoyable with someone else. However, it dawned on me that I needed to learn to enjoy being with myself as well, or else I would never know what it means to enjoy solitude; or my happiness could have possibly always been on the shoulders of someone else. And what if they simply didn't feel like it? Give yourself a chance to explore and see the things you never thought were possible.

And if you've sat and wallowed in work for a long time, how could you flip things? What amazing things can you do to see the reward in working hard? Perhaps you're in customer service or a similar role. Make the most of these moments to create memorable experiences with the people you come across. You may just be entertaining an angel in disguise. And if a trip or an experience just doesn't seem possible, a cheap way to make the most of life is to simply smile. It's scientifically proven that smiling can boost your immune system and boost your mood. If you have a hard time saying no to the things around you, find an excuse to get away and do something you'll enjoy, even for a little while. Take a day of rest or only work for half the day. This could be your way of making the most of what you have and journey to your happy place.

**prayer**

*Father, I thank you for what you're doing to help me think bigger so I can make the most of what you allow me to have and experience. I know that to get the most of something, I have to* go to the greatest extent. You want me to have what is great. As my Father, you're a great God who gives big gifts. Thank you! Open the eyes of my heart so that there's never a dull moment in this life while walking with you. Help me to see the joys in building, loving, working, serving, resting, and more. Help me to see YOU in it all. I value your presence in my life and I trust that you are granting me the wisdom needed to be fulfilled. Help me see the ways of escape, given by you, that allow me to make the most of opportunities in my life. Show me how to multiply a moment. As you gave Jesus the gift of multiplying things (Matthew 14:17–21), I trust that a similar gift is inside me. Show me how I can take what I have that may seem small and manifest it into something big. In Jesus's name, amen.

## scriptures to consider

Be very careful, then, how you live—not as unwise but as wise, making the most of every opportunity, because the days are evil. Therefore do not be foolish, but understand what the Lord's will is.

**EPHESIANS 5:15–17**

# CHAPTER 5

# Big and Bold

I remember being around eighteen years old, getting ready to put a new record out. As we were preparing the album cover, I noticed that out of all the photos that had been taken, the people at the recording company picked out the profile-like images. Face images. And if you look at my first records, you'll notice there were a lot of face images until I lost some weight.

During this point in my career, many people gave their opinion of what they thought was pretty. There was one exec I thought was on my side, however, and so I valued their opinion. They advised me to do my album covers the way the company wanted, and I did because I honestly believed this person was rooting for me. Then they told me someone said I needed to focus on my face because I looked like the Pillsbury Dough Boy. I never forgot it. It stung, but for some reason it didn't hurt me as badly as comments in reference to my weight had before, because it gave me the fire to begin accepting who I was and voicing more of what I wanted rather than letting others tell me what was best for me. This is also when I began to put up a fight for what I wanted, no matter what they thought was pretty. I no longer allowed people to sway me with heartless opinions that were only based on culture or a trend. Because I am no trend; I am a human being who was and is designed to perform and navigate the trend. I also began talking to myself and saying I would control the odds. I was determined to ride the wave of change, which in this case turned into body positivity, and not sink under someone else's negativity. I was OWNING IT!

As part of that decision, I decided to start eating better and losing some of the weight—not because it would make me look "prettier" and "more marketable," but because I wanted to better my health, and I wanted to lose weight *for me.* (Another reason I wanted to lose some of the weight is because I remember attempting to ride a roller coaster and the bar wouldn't go down. This is hilarious to me. However, it was unacceptable.) I decided this weight would not stop me from enjoying life. I began considering the other health risks that being overweight caused. And during this journey toward a healthier me both mentally and physically, I decided I wouldn't let others define "beauty" for me ever again. At this point, culture hadn't yet embraced the Big or Curvy woman, so I vocalized my challenges with getting the weight off and how it was also a reflection of my spiritual journey. I say it was a reflection of my spiritual journey because as I began to discipline myself with my eating habits, as the weight began to fall off, other dead weight—like relationships and poor ways of thinking—began to fall off. And during the entire process, I had made up my mind that I would still embrace a "healthy big"—when I began my weight-loss journey, I never intended to be a size 8 or 12. I mention all this to remind you to make changes for YOU. That even though I was a big girl, I had always been fly. Don't get it twisted! As part of this new confidence, I also began embracing the ideology, "If you're going to be big, wear it well." I wore the latest trends with confidence, and the guys who'd said they didn't date big girls were interested in me. I began to hear from my supporters and noticed my weight journey was a way of connecting with others who battled insecurities.

Maybe what they say about you isn't about the size you are; maybe they ostracize you because of your big personality, your big way of thinking, your big feet, your big mouth (they mentioned that about me too), your big family, or maybe your big gift that comes easy to you but not so easy for them. It's uncomfortable to deal with these comments because it's an attack on who we are, telling us we're somehow lacking or made wrong or just not acceptable. Which leads us to believe there really is something wrong with our makeup, something we'd do anything to change.

While I was dating a certain guy for a little while, he once got so angry with me that the only thing he could say while trying to resolve an issue between us was that I was a fat female dog. He mentioned I was big and unattractive. While I was very angry and hurt, I replied, "That's all you have on me, and you better believe that everything about me is big, and it's obviously something you're too small to handle." I hope you'll embrace the same way of thinking—that people speak from the places they are mentally, and we can't live according to the small-minded opinions of others. Because we can choose to grow and expand how we see ourselves—see the truth. I may be unattractively heavy in some people's eyes, but the glory on my life is heavy. My legacy is big. My money is big, and I have to be BIG enough to handle it.

I made something out of what was once an insecurity for me. I am doing what I can to maintain my temple, and I've created a clothing line centered around the thing many people try to hold against me. You have that same power to own the things that make you who you are—the things you value and love about yourself. You're a BIG deal and there's nothing wrong with that. And a lot of the time, the haters want to bring you down simply because what makes you "too big" is what makes you beautiful and amazingly different.

*Father, I thank you for the Bigness you have placed inside of me. Show me how to own and handle the gifts, talents, and differences you have given to me, since they are a part of me for a reason. Forgive me for ever doubting my makeup, as I am YOUR design. Going forward, strengthen me so I don't seek validation from anyone but you. Reveal me to myself—my true heart and how I'm truly feeling. Remove the learned behaviors I've taken on to protect or hide myself. Transform my mind (Romans 12:2) and show me how to define beauty differently than the world, so I strive for what you see as beautiful. And help me grow in my understanding of your glory and how you see me, so I can see you. Once I see you, I'll know my vision is different. Allow me to be bold about what I see, and help me identify who you have called me to be on earth. Father, give me the confidence I need to walk upright and with peace. I come against the facade of happiness. I will not put on a mask to hide what's true for me. I will live out loud, and my truth to the world will be my truth from you! Give me the courage to be bold with what you've given me and the discipline to correct what you haven't. In Jesus's name, I pray. Amen.*

"I have told you these things, so that in me you may have peace. In this world you will have trouble. But take heart! I have overcome the world."

**JOHN 16:33**

I praise you because I am fearfully and wonderfully made; your works are wonderful, I know that full well.

**PSALM 139:14**

# CHAPTER 6

# Don't Rush Your Process

Things will happen little by little. A good example of this is how God dealt with the children of Israel—making them wait until they were prepared and ready for the work and blessings to come in the promised land. Once I learned the characteristics of God shown in that story, I understood him better. I moved different. And once I better grasped God's timing, I was less shaken by life when I didn't understand him or why something wasn't happening for me yet.

Though God is supernatural, he's into developmental processes. He can definitely make everything happen at one time, but instead he often takes his time and makes rational decisions, letting us make our own choices along the way to ensure all parts of the puzzle are in place. He knows when we are honestly ready for the end goal. He also knows we will sometimes say we are ready out of impatience, when really there's a piece of the puzzle we've not found yet—a piece we will need in place in order to take on a challenge when it matters.

There are lessons we must learn in order to not repeat the same mistakes in our own promised lands. Have you ever had to repeat the same lesson over and over again? I have. I know it gets frustrating, but the lesson must be revisited until we get it!

An example is one of my relationships. I had been prophesied to about how it wasn't a good fit, time and time again. (Remember the conversation with Courtney in chapter 2?) But I wanted to be with this guy because I loved him so much, and I had already given so much of myself to him—I was determined to make it work. I just didn't have it in me to break up with him or to simply walk away. Well, actually, I would break up with him, but I would go right back to him if he called. I carried on that way for so long. The message I received wasn't just about him not being the right person for me; it was also that I wasn't the right person for him. I simply wasn't ready to listen.

During this time, I also learned I wasn't trusting God as much as I said I did. I was walking in rebellion, taking things into my own hands by basically living with this man and acting like we were married. Ladies, playing house is a dangerous thing. The lesson in this was to never play wife to a boyfriend. Since I ignored what God's will was for my life, I continued to get hurt and disappointed. I was hoping it would be different each time this guy and I got back together, but it never changed. During this time, God made it a priority for me to get the message of what was best for my life. I began journaling, and noticed I learned a lesson—the same lesson—every time, but even then I was not willing to let the guy go quite yet. I would ask my friends, "Am I stupid for going back?" Some would say in the nice way that I was. While this feedback helped me, my big breakthrough wasn't until I'd officially had enough and I came across a scripture I'd never really paid attention to, Proverbs 26:11: "As a dog returns to its vomit, so fools repeat their folly." In that moment, it was like God was saying, "Yes, boo, you're very silly for going back . . ." God and I often have some really funny moments together.

I kept writing in my journal and finally began to truly realize this relationship was not good for me. That it couldn't be what God had planned for me. Especially as I would get so hurt that it literally began making me sick. I would cry so hard I'd become nauseous and have headaches. I would confess to myself that this wasn't the life I wanted. I literally began regurgitating a hard truth that I didn't want to accept because this man was fine and we had a sexual relationship that was clouding my mind. I began realizing that I wanted it to turn around for my good without letting anything go—and it truly was turning around for me, but in a horrible way. Clear evidence began to pile up that I wasn't the end all be all for him.

Confession: During this time, I was in a hurry to be married and I wanted to force this one to be my husband. If God had left it up to me, I would probably been married and divorced three times by now due to poor choices. So even though I knew better, and God had told me better, I continued to go back and invest in what was hurting me. In doing that, I noticed I was like the scriptural analogy, returning to what I knew wasn't good for me. And while I was trying to rush the process with this man, I kept getting frustrated. Things weren't turning out the way I wanted them to, even in my career, because my need to sort everything out quickly was affecting my entire life. When it came to building my record, for instance, my brother would annoy me with the question, "Why are you so in a hurry?" He didn't know that was a loaded question. And as my frustrations grew and the reason behind them became more evident, I had my family and friends constantly side-eyeing me when it came to this relationship. Unfortunately, I had such a hard head that I stayed just so they wouldn't be right. I wanted to be right about my own life. However, I had to learn that the Lord sends people to give us answers and there's absolutely nothing wrong with that.

While I was repeating the same lesson over and over again, I certainly wasted a lot of time, but I can honestly say it did a lot for my development and future choices. God allowed me to no longer look at everyone else's life and think my timeline had to match theirs for it to be good. Because everything in his timing is good. He challenged me to not rush things because he was still developing things in me. You ever seen someone who is always in a hurry but never going anywhere—like rushing out of the house, but having to go back because they forgot their wallet? This is what it looks like when you rush your God-ordained process. Some of us have to endure a thorough process to ensure we have everything with us for the next destination—and in this relationship, I didn't have everything I needed to thrive. Had I kept moving any longer and without God, I certainly would have left so much of my future potential behind.

I finally surrendered to the Lord, left the relationship for good, and began playing the game as a single woman. I saw I didn't need to be with someone else to enjoy life. I took it one day at a time. When I flirted, I kept my standards. When I made mistakes, I didn't stay there for too long. And after I'd slowed down and prioritized my life, I bumped into Jordan, who became my fiancé (and possibly my husband by the time you're reading this). At that point I'd decided I wouldn't allow certain things from my past to happen to me again. So if there were any signs of what I'd seen before or any red flags, I committed to getting out of there! I didn't give room for the "benefit of the doubt." Blah, blah! I wasn't going through the heartbreak again. I'd also promised myself that, from that point on, anyone I committed to had to make sense. A hard truth is that "slowing down" is a part of the process. In order to make a safe turn, you have to slow down. One day at church, for some reason, Jordan looked super handsome to me. He had been in my life since we were kids, through our families and our church, but we went our separate ways during high school and college. We started dating, and he was very clear about what he wanted. I never had any questions about where we were going. He made sure I didn't. We were both very honest about our lives and prior experiences as well. Although he took too long to approach me, once he did, we never fell out of touch. We fell in love. Our relationship was so easy and peaceful. Even the arguments were different. It was going so good, and whenever we realized how fast it was going, we'd slow down and do frequent self-checks to make sure we were good with the speed; and we kept agreeing we felt safe to continue. There was no uncertainty. I think we both had been in seasons in our lives when we were too involved and getting ourselves in God's way. So, when we looked up, we were surprised at how smooth things were going, how much we loved each other, and how good it was. There was a rest that we shared while in our relationship, and a feeling that we had reached a safe destination sooner than we thought, even though we were taking things slow. This is what assured me that God was in it.

I have cried at the thought of Jordan's presence in my life. His presence is like a clear sign of God reminding me that he had me all along, but I simply needed to slow down to let myself become the woman I needed to be to take on the life he had in mind. My parents, who are my natural and spiritual covering, gave me their blessing, something I once thought was too good to be true. Unfortunately, this is what the enemy wants us to believe. He wants us to believe we have to suffer through something before any good comes out of it. However, this isn't true. Anything that comes from the Lord is good, and it is our Father's desire for us to have what is good and healthy. Don't rush it! Take your time. Pay attention to the lessons God sends and learn from them. You will see that God has you.

**prayer**

*Father, help me to trust your timing. Forgive me for not always trusting you and ignoring your instruction, taking it upon myself to force what I want. I see now you're more concerned with what I need and not just what I want, because sometimes my wants are driven by how I am feeling and the place that I am in during that moment. But you supply me with what I need based off of what you see in my days to come. Father, please continue developing me into the woman you want me to be. Help me embrace and own my process. Though you may be working little by little, remind me that you know what I can digest. And when I get impatient, please just send me a reminder that you've got me. Help me understand that it is okay for things to happen when you approve. Help me to be okay with it happening for me, and in me, "little by little." Amen.*

As a dog returns to its vomit, so fools repeat their folly.

**PROVERBS 26:11**

But I will not drive them out in a single year, because the land would become desolate and the wild animals too numerous for you. Little by little I will drive them out before you, until you have increased enough to take possession of the land.

**EXODUS 23:29–30**

# CHAPTER 7

# The Silver Spoon

The silver spoon is an English expression associated with wealth. Inherited wealth. It comes from the fact that in the 1700s, spoons were often carried around like a passport or a driver's license, identifying the social class you came from and that you belonged at the table. And for most of my life, I've met people who believe I was born with a silver spoon because of who my family is.

I remember being teased that I didn't know "the struggle" because my parents were in a different financial state than some of my friends. An old friend of mine continuously mentioned I didn't know what it was like to work hard. I tried to give them the benefit of the doubt by believing they meant I didn't know what it felt like to do hard physical labor. I didn't want to believe someone I called a friend was minimizing what I did—working in the recording industry. Because the truth is, I did have to make my way to get where I am now, since nobody handed me success. And what I do as an occupation seems easy to some, but it is definitely hard work. Honestly, it is quite taxing on the body. But because I'm working with purpose, it often feels easy, or it is fun! However, am I at fault for living in purpose and enjoying what I do? Should work feel like "work"? Doesn't God make the way easy for the righteous? Isn't that what God's favor is about?

Over time, I became tired of giving people the benefit of the doubt. I began taking what people said and paying attention to it. If I'm being considerate enough to think twice, then shouldn't they? They obviously mean what they say. People will make you feel like you're stuck up or sadiddy for wanting to make the best decisions for yourself, your family, or maybe your children now or to come. If you're in this space, don't feel bad for wanting something different and following a different path. Don't feel bad for the favor that is on your life. Check your goals. Ask yourself if they're unrealistic. Sometimes how society says things should be is not how God says it should be for you. Or maybe people are saying it's too easy for you, but you and God understand and know otherwise. Many of us are operating in survival mode while others truly believe God and operate in faith and love. But no matter what, it's the hustle and belief in yourself and God, not the perspiration you put in for the sake of "working hard," that counts. I have learned that what God puts in our hearts is often too big for the average person to believe. There's insight we have as believers that is often not easy to fathom or interpret. God will give you a dream that some may say, "Whoa! That's not possible!" But when it comes to anything with God, if it's in his will, is certainly possible. And even if they see that what you're working toward is obtainable, they may still try to talk you down from it, but don't let that make you feel unsure about what you're walking in. WALK IN IT!

And just because you're an entrepreneur or someone successful, that doesn't mean you don't have someone to answer to. Just because you're in customer service doesn't mean you aren't succeeding. God made us all servants. If you work a nine-to-five, it doesn't make you less than or greater than. As believers, we're all doing everything we do as if it's us serving God directly. First Corinthians 10:31 says, "So whether you eat or drink or whatever you do, do it all for the glory of God." Take on the spirit of service. There are many pieces to the puzzle, and if any of them are missing, the picture won't be complete. You are what makes the world go round. If corporations give their employees raises and bonuses, then why wouldn't your God do it for you? In fact, God is a giver of spoons.

Psalm 112 says that wealth and riches are in your Father's house if you delight in him. So I like to carry my silver spoon—the sign of my blessings—with me. You've inherited this kind of living too! Own it! And when asking for a few more spoons, request however many you want! Go after a gold or platinum spoon trimmed in diamonds. You shouldn't strive for anything less-than. If people say you're spoiled, so what. Embrace God's favor on your life. Enjoy the fact you are one of God's children. Don't feel bad about what he is doing for you. Don't be ashamed of the favor that is on your life. If you get a new car, don't tiptoe around people. If you get a new home, don't minimize it for the sake of others. Be wise with what you show for safety, but certainly don't silence the loud-doing or the big-livin' in your life. Live out loud and let your life be the voice of God to someone else that says, "It can happen for you!" Have someone to share it with and get excited alongside you. God didn't call us to operate in dysfunction, so you shouldn't feel at fault for having things in order or wanting better for yourself and doing it in a way the world doesn't understand.

Your spoons aren't about material things, but accepting them is about owning who your Father is and not feeling bad for people who don't trust God enough to work on their behalf. You may say I'm wrong, but give them something to talk about. I challenge you to say to others who don't celebrate you, or to the adversary, "I own the fact God has favored me, and you won't make me feel bad for giving my life to Christ and seeing the results from it." Which means not walking with a sense of entitlement but being appreciative of the fact your life could be different.

Allow God's glory on your life to be a beacon of light to the world and to others around you. It'll attract some to want to know your God, and it'll cause some to question you. At the end of the day, we all get a spoon. What you decide to do with it is what will make the difference.

_____**prayer**

*Father, thank you for your favor. Thank you for the opportunities you have given me that I didn't "work" for, as well as the ones I did fight to achieve. I am grateful that you protect me, you cover me, and you're always sending me unexpected surprises. I receive and accept your rich blessings and will not apologize for what you're doing for me. Thank you for allowing me to be clear in my purpose and operating within that. Help me to focus on where I should be so I'm not unhappy in an occupation that isn't best for your plan. I believe you will whisper my name to the right resources, and I trust you're working on my behalf and making the way clear. You are putting my name first when I had placed it there last. Thank you for trusting me with the moments you give. I remember you said in your Word, Matthew 7:11, "If you, then . . . know how to give good gifts to your children, how much more will your Father in heaven give good gifts to those who ask him!" You are a good Father and I am grateful for your mercy and the gifts you've bestowed upon me and my family. Amen.*

For you bless the righteous, O Lord; you cover him with favor as with a shield.

**PSALM 5:12 (ESV)**

Let the favor of the Lord our God be upon us, and establish the work of our hands upon us; yes, establish the work of our hands!

**PSALM 90:17 (ESV)**

In times of disaster they will not wither; in days of famine they will enjoy plenty.

**PSALM 37:19**

# Blessings on Blessings

As I was studying how God's favor works, I discovered that he'll bless others for your sake because he favors you. Genesis 39:2–6 lays it out so well! Verse 2 says, "The Lord greatly blessed Joseph there in the home of his master, so that everything he did succeeded" (TLB). And Potiphar noticed it! So Joseph naturally became quite a favorite with him. Soon, Joseph—who at that time was the lowest of servants—was put in charge of the administration and care of Potiphar's business affairs. Genesis 39:5 says, "At once the Lord began blessing Potiphar for *Joseph's sake*. All his household affairs began to run smoothly, his crops *flourished*, and his flocks *multiplied*. So Potiphar gave Joseph the complete administrative responsibility over *everything* he owned" (TLB, italics mine). Joseph, by the way, is noted as a very handsome young man as well, which is often called out with the men God highly favored.

Be bold and beautiful while enjoying God's favor, and spread those blessings to the others around you as well.

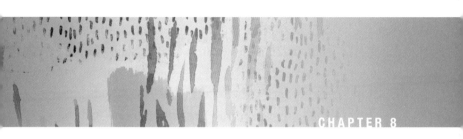

# CHAPTER 8

# Stop Comparing Yourself

In the beginning stages of my career, I had dreamt of accomplishing several things, and I hadn't yet seen the full vision of what I thought was "success." So I started questioning the vision God had given me. I began looking at others and saying, "It's happening for them, but why not for me?" The comparison started turning into a hint of jealousy. I soon became so overwhelmed with comparing myself that I lost sight of what exactly I was called to do. It was like driving fast but always looking to my left, never looking forward. I began to get confused when it came to my purpose in life. I said I was inspired by someone else but, in all honesty, I began looking too much at them and not seeing me. While watching others water their flowers, weeds began to grow around mine, hence choking the life out of my assignment, much like the parable of the sower and the weeds in Matthew 13:22. In those verses, "the seed falling among the thorns refers to someone who hears the word, but the worries of this life and the deceitfulness of wealth choke the word, making it unfruitful." In the same way, the promise God had given me began to lose its voice in my life because I began wanting the success that "they" had.

Later, I had an awakening. I realized no one had the power to be me. And this realization was powerful, because it also shows that very often, we are pointing the finger at the enemy when in reality our weeds come up because of our own choices, not making the most of an opportunity, ignoring the signs, etc. My choice is my power. How I see myself, what I do with my time and my words, shapes my world. I am God's handiwork. He gave ME dominion. Surely, he wouldn't make something with no value or give gifts for no reason. My mother once said, "Everything that God does, he does it well." I had to change my mindset and then believe it.

Everything he has created has life and the ability to grow. So, sister, grow and love on yourself. Water yourself with the Word of God and see what he is doing through *you*. See what he is doing for *you*. Isaiah 43:19 says, "See, I am doing a new thing! Now it springs up; do you not perceive it? I am making a way in the wilderness and streams in the wasteland." No one else has the power to be you. You can win the fight against despair, rejection, insecurity, or heaviness, because you're not fighting the battle alone. God is there, and he'll send what you need to carry through.

_____**prayer**

*Father, help me make good decisions. Help me to see your glory being revealed in and through me. Transform my mind and remove any lies that have carried the weight of self-sabotaging ideas. Help me to genuinely celebrate others, be inspired, and be unintimidated by what you're doing through and for them. Remove jealousy and doubt from my heart and mind so that no one has to fall for me to go up. Dismantle that way of thinking. Help me see the uniqueness you've created in me. Make my purpose clear to me. Help me with time management, so that I am busy minding my business and don't have the time to compare myself to anyone else. Give me the security and certainty of who I am in you, your kingdom, and on the earth. Push back the darkness of depression or insecurity. Amen.*

_____**scriptures to consider**

Jesus told them another parable: "The kingdom of heaven is like a man who sowed good seed in his field. But while everyone was sleeping, his enemy came and sowed weeds among the wheat, and went away. When the wheat sprouted and formed heads, then the weeds also appeared. The owner's servants came to him and said, 'Sir, didn't you sow good seed in your field? Where then did the weeds come from?' 'An enemy did this,' he replied."

MATTHEW 13:24–28

Each one should test their own actions. Then they can take pride in themselves alone, without comparing themselves to someone else, for each one should carry their own load. Nevertheless, the one who receives instruction in the word should share all good things with their instructor.

GALATIANS 6:4–6

# CHAPTER 9

# God as My Agent

I am honestly seeing that the work pays off. In 2018, I closed a deal with Macy's for Eleven60 and I still cannot believe it. I am so grateful for the opportunity. And I am completely in awe of what God does on my behalf, and know he will do the same for you.

Recognize what you have when you've got it! I kept looking at other people and saying, "Why is it taking me so long to get there?" until I realized my infrastructure wasn't ready for my wild dreams. I remember praying for Macy's. I had big plans for what I could do there. But I was always stuck in the planning stage or hitting a wall—because I wanted to be in stores immediately with no steps in between. In fact, my big Macy's opportunity only happened because my cousin

LaKisha had been inspired to send me a link, encouraging me to sign up for the possibility of joining their Workshop, a program that would help me get a better handle on my brand so I could get my clothing line off the ground.

I'm sure many of us have those moments where we overlook certain links because of the scams that are floating around. I'll be honest, I was a bit slow to sign up because I didn't know how real it was. However, this one wasn't a scam. Next thing I knew, God did it! Out of one thousand submissions, I was one of the ten people chosen. This is with no recognition of my name. No manager signed me up for this. No PR or agent got me a spot. It was all God and the persistence that God put in me! Macy's said we had to fly out to New York, and I did just that with no hesitation. Shamika and I flew out to learn what they had to teach. We sat in the workshops and asked all the questions we could think of. It was made very clear to us that this program was only meant to give us more information on retail and merchandising. They said numerous times there was no promise we'd be in stores— website or physical. But we were given the opportunity to sit in front of major department heads within this major corporation, and that was all I needed. I remained a student.

Toward the end of this experience, they began discussing the possibility of Shamika and me pitching to Macy's representatives. Right around this time I was in the season where people were coming and going in the Eleven60 office. We hadn't yet figured it all out. The team wasn't as solid as I would've liked it to be. On the Workshop itinerary, there was a scheduled pop-up shop that called for buyers and everyday customers to come into one of their flagship stores, with the Workshop attendees' products on the floor. We basically had to sell and pitch that we had a product worth having in their store. God was with us and the pitch went well. So many people came out to support the brand. In the end, we did 50 percent of all sales. I was blown away. I went back to my hotel room completely overwhelmed with all kinds of emotions. I felt like I had won a marathon that I had been dreaming of entering for years. I kept thanking God for the opportunity.

I share this with you to encourage you to remember that as long as we walk upright with the Lord, he will make a way for us. I have heard my father say, "God will make a way out of no way." God did just that. Shamika and I got back home, and we received a call saying we had an opportunity to sell on Macy's website. God did that! I knew I had a product to offer. And God knew the Workshop was what I needed so I could take on the real work and handle it well—and that the website placement would also grow me and prepare me for going into stores.

For a long time, the enemy made suggestions, having me believe success would never happen. Or that I needed certain people to walk in certain doors and decide to boost my business. Don't get me wrong; God will use people to bless us. However, sometimes God will work on our behalf so that no human will get the glory, and instead it will be clear it was all by divine purpose.

*Father, thank you for what you're doing in my life. I thank you for your grace and your mercy. Thank you for your favor. I ask that you allow me to have peace in you. And, Lord, thank you for this confidence you've allowed me to have because of your works and your faithfulness. I thank you for being in my future. I'm grateful you're having conversations with people, through people, about me. Thank you for the open doors you're allowing me to walk into. I trust you will connect me with who I need to be connected to in order to fulfill your purpose for me on the earth. Remove anything that can block the level of sensitivity that is necessary to discern and see. Increase my level of creativity and hold me accountable so that I am constantly moving with you. If there is a shift, show me how to move with you. Whatever it takes, I want to be where you are. Where you are, are solutions, strength, peace, and clarity. Life makes sense when you're in it! Amen.*

Let the favor of the Lord our God be upon us, and establish the work of our hands upon us; yes, establish the work of our hands!

**PSALM 90:17 (ESV)**

Since ancient times no one has heard, no ear has perceived, no has seen any God besides you, who acts in behalf of those who wait for him.

**ISAIAH 64:4**

CHAPTER 10

# Pick Up the Pieces and Grab the Glue

Aglass that is broken or shattered can't hold liquid or contain anything solid. "Make sure you aren't asking for a solid situation while in a broken state," I'd tell myself. But I didn't always follow my own advice when it came to dating and love. It took a lot of soul-searching and time for me to be in a place I could receive the solid relationship I was searching for.

Sometimes, we'll ask God for something so great and refreshing while not having asked, "God, where am I in this season of my life?" Or, "What do I look like to you? Am I in good condition?" And these are questions we can also ask our safe friends, parents, or anyone we trust who knows us well—as well as ask ourselves. A healthy woman is one who can honestly take advice and evaluate herself to see if she is ready for the desire she may have in her heart. When I started looking honestly at myself, I learned I had become so broken and conditioned by poor behaviors that I only knew how to evaluate others and not myself. And as a result, I discovered why I hadn't been able to learn from my past or the good examples around me.

I noticed my father's security and desire to protect his family. I noticed my mother's grace and desire to build her home. But I became hesitant to build with anyone because I focused on the pain I encountered from outside. And while I had been taught that a good man appreciates a woman who has grace and is okay with him filling his role in the relationship, at one point in my life I was trying to be it all—strong, powerful, and tough like a man—and I wasn't graceful when dealing with people who had nothing to do with my past hurt. I kept disguising my fears while making others feel like they were responsible for them. I told myself, "You need to find your grace where you left it. Deal with that place. Walk away from it but don't leave any pieces of yourself behind." But I wasn't listening to myself. I was traveling to the promised place broken, arriving with only shards of me left. Hence, it made new relationships difficult. I had no hope for good experiences. I became immune to hurt, and as I grew older, I knew this condition wasn't good for me if I one day wanted to raise a child or be a wife. I had to ask the Lord to put me back together and help me clothe myself again with the garment of praise and grace rather than the garment of despair.

I'll be honest—because I had been so broken, I often turned off people who were my solution or way of help. Whether it be the place you've been praying for or the relationship you've been praying for, there are some things you must understand about yourself first. You need to own the behaviors you have learned and decide to unlearn them so that the good people or new places aren't having to pay penalty fees. It's like when we rent a car. The rental company rep walks around the car with you to see if there are any dents. If there are dents from the previous driver, the new driver doesn't pay for them. It's the same with us. Sometimes we need to ask ourselves, "Who's been driving me?" Don't make the new driver pay for the last driver. Meaning you shouldn't come with baggage or dents from previous situations.

And as much as possible, we need to deal with the damage head on. Have you ever seen someone who had it made, but because they had a drug habit, they destroyed everything? While some of us may not do drugs, and frown upon the drug addict, we're often in the same boat, because our protective mechanisms become an addiction and a tool that damages new relationships or even the new places we are in. For example, imagine developing anger problems over time and your usual becomes throwing vases or breaking glasses and things. I became this person. Never saw it in my home as a child, but I picked it up in a dysfunctional relationship and from watching reality TV. Once you're in a new relationship or space, just like moving into a new home, those damages will cost you more to fix later than if you dealt with them before you agreed to purchase the property. So in order to not have to pay for those issues, we must change our behaviors.

No one wants to take on damaging behaviors. Just like sometimes we don't have the patience to deal with certain people. Can you commit to the hard work of addressing your broken places, or will you be a nagging woman, the woman who is never satisfied with the people or the place you have been praying for, or who looks for ways to protect yourself so you don't get hurt first? How often do you desire for someone to love you the way you need to be loved? How stressful is it for them to not be able to love you simply because you're so broken or fearful?

This isn't even about a man at this point. It's more so about who you and I have become as individuals. Are we gentle? Are we open to the solutions, or the "better," that God may be sending our way? Are we unmanageable? We're called to focus on growing in Christ so we're ready for a life in heaven. What things must we master while here on earth?

_____**prayer**

*Father, prepare me for my future. I ask that you come into my heart and deliver me from the damaging behaviors and ways of protecting myself while entering into this safe place you have promised me, or that I have been praying for. Help me walk in grace and own it. Remove what I think is strong and develop in me the strength that comes from you. Help me heal so that I am not pushing away great opportunities for my career, love life, or lifetime friendships. Allow me to be so secure in you, I'm not forcing what I think should be there. Forgive me for asking for my desires, being impatient, but not realizing that I was too broken to handle it. I now give to you what I can't handle, instead of acting like I have it under control. I'll own where I am weak, because the strength you're giving me, I'll be proud to own. I trust that you are "completing your work in me," because I don't think you'd want me in heaven with so much weight. Help me to see my issues and take ownership to grow into the woman I am called to be. In your name I pray. Amen.*

_____scriptures to consider

Therefore, if anyone is in Christ, he is a new creation. The old has passed away; behold, the new has come.

**2 CORINTHIANS 5:17–18 (ESV)**

He heals the brokenhearted and binds up their wounds.

**PSALM 147:3**

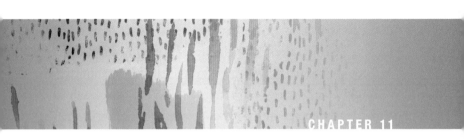

# CHAPTER 11

# Doing It God's Way

I can only imagine how God feels after having told me multiple times to do something one way and I've done the complete opposite. He told us not to have sex out of wedlock because of the emotional attachment we develop over time. It's sad, because experience had to be my teacher with this one. As I said before, for years I couldn't let go of someone because I was in a situation that made me feel like a wife to someone temporary. While involving myself in premarital sex, during that moment I felt wanted or desired. Unfortunately, I had forgotten that sex was not the solution to what needed to be communicated. I was broken. Going from relationship to relationship wasn't helping me. I would feel put back together again for a moment but a slow rise of guilt, shame, and the memories of why I was making these choices rested right there with me. This then added to my warfare. The enemy began using MY poor decisions against me. Condemnation was a part of my battle. I began realizing that this is exactly why sex is considered an act of worship for marriage and not for single life. It is designed for a safe and committed place. When we wait until we're committed to someone in marriage, the relationship is not one-sided, and we can depend on the other person considering us, not just themselves. We can trust that a man of God will understand a woman is giving her most prized possession, and what she does with it is her answer to God and to who she chooses to love. We can trust that our partner's decisions aren't only based off his feelings, but that he has considered what God thinks of him.

When I started practicing celibacy, I learned I was far clearer and able to see how that person treated me. I was able to discern character versus nature. I then was able to see if a behavior was something they would actually change, or if it was simply who they were. It was no longer me attempting to change a man, or me waiting on a man to change. Guys who are big brothers or uncles to me have always said that a man will change for who he wants. I didn't believe them, but now that I have met Jordan, I've learned that it is very true. Jordan is the most disciplined man I've dealt with concerning this. I never prayed with a man as part of our regimen in a relationship. But here I am, not perfect, but praying with Jordan and having Christ at the center of our relationship. Jordan mentioned to me before, "I don't want our relationship to be based solely on sex." Being with him has brought light to my life. I realized I was making decisions based off physical things instead of using my brain. In the past there were times when I couldn't get to Jesus, and neither could a man I was sleeping with. What a dangerous place! Things began to get complicated in my life because I had completely taken this part of it into my own hands. Had I stayed a virgin and waited until marriage, I wouldn't have based decisions off something that isn't the foundation of marriage, and things that don't sustain a marriage. I kept moving based off my feelings, and feelings pass.

Sex isn't the end all, be all. Had I not had sex or started a body count, that part of a relationship never would have mattered to me. How often do we add to the problems of a future marriage because we have no discipline? Imagine being a woman married to a man who had multiple partners—how would you feel? What worries would go through your mind about your relationship, or thoughts of comparison? Because when you or your partner have been with someone (or multiple someones), those thoughts happen, with our imaginations driving us to a place of whether or not we are good enough, causing us to make decisions that will only add to the mental war. What if instead we were to really try and do it God's way and trust his wisdom? Could things be better? Could you be giving the world one more successful marriage or secure woman?

It was evident I made poor choices with the most

intimate part of my being while not considering my soul. It was like I was giving spiritual wolves permission to enter my home, when God's plan was for me to never be robbed in that way. And while at the time I felt my decisions added to my adult conversations, there is so much unnecessary hurt I still dealt with. I now admit, if I had done it God's way, there's so much I could have avoided!

Make better decisions with the people you allow into your life. If we train our bodies to consume expired milk or foods, it'll respond negatively the first time, but if we continue, we'll become immune to the poisons. How often have we tolerated expired relationships? As a result, we've learned behaviors that causes us not to respond, to respond in a dysfunctional way, or even to believe the right kind of love isn't actually out there somewhere for us.

_____**prayer**

*Father, help me to have a clear mind and not destroy what you have planned for my future. Strengthen me so I am able to detach myself from what isn't good for me. Show me how I can get closer to you. I give you full authority to have your way in my life. I submit to you. I surrender to you. Father, though I may have gotten into some things that were outside of your will, I now want your will. I trust you want what's best for me. I trust that you know what's better for me. Please cleanse me from the negative ties I've connected myself with while not being in your authorized territory. Please deliver me from anything that will jeopardize my future and deliver me from anything that would cause me to stay broken. Please forgive me for my sins. Come into my heart and continue to transform me. Amen.*

_____**scriptures to consider**

How can a young person stay on the path of purity? By living according to your word.

**PSALM 119:9**

"I have the right to do anything," you say—but not everything is beneficial. "I have the right to do anything"—but I will not be mastered by anything.

**1 CORINTHIANS 6:12**

Commit your actions to the Lord, and your plans will succeed.

**PROVERBS 16:3 (NLT)**

# CHAPTER 12

# Successfully Single

I've had to grow up and learn that every woman who is single isn't miserable. And that your relationship status doesn't define your value or level of wisdom. Some of us are single by choice and not because we're not "wanted."

The level of focus and freedom that came once I accepted my singleness was quite liberating. To be without the pressure of feeling the need to have a man is beyond refreshing. Did I always want to walk it alone? Not necessarily. (Maybe for you, it's different.) I do still believe in marriage, compromise, and love; I just no longer think that being single is the worst thing in the world. For me, being single meant time to become secure and to discover my security wasn't dependent on anyone else. It allowed me the opportunity to no longer take what someone else did as a personal attack, and I began walking with a new sense of peace because I accepted their actions weren't about me. Instead, those actions spoke about the other person. If you were a cheat, you were a cheat. Simple. I no longer gave it the authority to say I was less-than.

As I embraced the years of my singleness, I played the game and didn't feel bad for beginning to play it so well. I owned it! Hence, I became most fulfilled when I embraced my singleness. I didn't put my life on hold in order to experience it with a man, or anyone else. Which is something I hadn't done in the past . . . I even paid for boyfriends to come on a trip, attempting to expose them to greater things, and in the end they wouldn't show up or destroyed the clarity of the trip. Had I been whole, I would not have allowed the disrespect to go so far. I would have been clear on what love will and won't do. And the reason I wanted to share this truthful moment is because I have seen so many young women put their lives on hold simply to wait on their boyfriend. Know your worth and your voice! Value doesn't beg. You, sister, are of great value, but you've got to know it and own it before anybody else.

My new level of surrender to God also gave me the confidence within myself to know that whether a husband came or not, I was good. And to know that when he came, I wouldn't feel lost or imprisoned by the other possibilities of "what I could've had." I got to a place I was whole and mature enough to be content with my decision to stay single until the right time came. And now that I have found my future husband, marriage won't feel like a prison or something my happiness depends on; it'll simply feel like a covenant between two humans who are in love. I thought I was ready for marriage when I was twenty, but now I see that I wasn't. It took the days of my singleness for me to find successful development, embracing the beautiful gifts God gave women to offer to the world. I began realizing there was a power that had been dormant in me because I was focused on so many other things. I owned the ability that God had given me to nurture, create, and transform. This realization moved me to take care of myself to ensure I brought good fruit into the world.

Will you contemplate giving up the single life sometimes? Maybe! It can be tempting to go after a guy who looks good in the moment but isn't for the long-term, or someone who is promising things he may not be able to deliver. But God's timing will change your perspective if you're open to it. Singleness has enlightened me to who I am and who I am not because I've had opportunities to grow and work on myself. Unfortunately, a lot of women don't give themselves time to learn who they are before marriage. Now their marriage feels like a life sentence. In fact, I used to think a single woman couldn't tell a married woman anything because they weren't seasoned enough. However, it all depends on the kind of single woman that the advice comes from. If she's godly and wise, she may share better ideas than the married woman when it comes to life and relationships, because she's had different experiences along the way.

Have you been successful in making a covenant with yourself? Sometimes we stay stuck loving the first person we fall in love with because we've not opened ourselves up to other opportunities. Sometimes we are single because this generation's man isn't always compatible with this generation's kind of woman. What time and love do you need to give to *yourself*?

Make a commitment not to play house or focus on whether or not someone is loving you back. Every single woman isn't unhappy, and being single doesn't mean she isn't desired. Some single women aren't married because they're a different breed of woman or they discover they're simply happy all by themselves. Or at the least, they grow in ways they wouldn't have otherwise. As a result, singleness may become one of the most liberating seasons in your life. There's a level of peace and maturity that is needed in being true to ourselves, and for any future relationship like marriage when it's time.

Embrace your singleness and discover who you are. Own this journey and let God walk you through it.

_____**prayer**

*Father, don't allow me to fabricate who I am and what is honestly in my heart. Allow me to walk with you and to let my presence around others be refreshing simply because of my time* and communion with you. I ask that you give me the tenacity and the tools to not be knocked off of my square. Give me confidence so I can walk with my head high. Don't allow me to rush to a man, or to an opportunity that I thought was from you because I wanted to see what wasn't there. Help me to know when it is you, so that I can own the decisions I make. Don't allow me to fill a void. Help me not to get caught up on the ideas of this world but do life for me so that I can leave this world with you, Jesus. Give me the discipline to seek the beauty and transformation that can take place in a season of singleness. Amen.

## scriptures to consider

Daughters of Jerusalem, I charge you by the gazelles and by the does of the field: Do not arouse or awaken love until it so desires.

**SONG OF SONGS 2:7**

Charm is deceptive, and beauty is fleeting; but a woman who fears the Lord is to be praised.

**PROVERBS 31:30**

I want you to be free from anxieties. The unmarried man is anxious about the things of the Lord, how to please the Lord. But the married man is anxious about worldly things, how to please his

wife, and his interests are divided. And the unmarried or betrothed woman is anxious about the things
of the Lord, how to be holy in body and spirit. But
the married woman is anxious about worldly things,
how to please her husband. I say this for your own
benefit, not to lay any restraint upon you, but to
promote good order and to secure your undivided
devotion to the Lord.

1 CORINTHIANS 7:32–35 (ESV)

# CHAPTER 13

# Past Mistakes Don't Determine Your Future

**W**e all have things we desperately want, and choices we've made to put that future in action ourselves. Sometimes not-so-great choices. And if you're anything like me, you may wonder if your trying so hard to make it work has messed things up so much, your dreams will never happen in the future as a result.

One of the things I've struggled with wanting to make happen is having my own family. And that desire affected my dating life and decision-making for a while. Before I got engaged in 2020, I honestly considered having a surrogate carry for me or moving forward with one of the poor choices of men I'd dated. For you, it might not be babies or wanting to start a family, but I'm sure there's something you desire that is causing you to take things into your own hands and even silence the voice in your heart that says what you're doing isn't what God really wants for you. It's just hard to listen when you want it so badly.

And like we've looked at in earlier chapters, sometimes we trick ourselves into thinking we're ready because of what we see around us—the comparison trap is a hard one to escape in so many parts of our lives. For example, while I was looking at how everyone else was progressing in love and with children, I would easily say, "I should have that" or "I'm ready for that." However, the question I needed to ask was, "Am I really ready for this?" And "Is my plan the best idea to make it happen?" Children come into the restroom while you're on the toilet. They don't respect your privacy. Just consider, my four-year-old niece Kali and I will be in one room, and then both walk in on my mother while she's using the restroom or getting dressed, as if this is what my mother should deem as normal. Imagine if it were you, and a four-year-old is creating a play space on the floor near you while you're trying to use the restroom, and a woman in her thirties is leaning on the counter asking you life questions at the same time. Mommy manages it so well, but that's because her maturity, wisdom, and connection kicks in, helping her to discern if this is a time when she tells us to get out or one when she simply embraces our desire or need for her voice. Am I ready for that level of commitment and discernment?

Are you ready for a life-changing event? Building and training human beings, or whatever it is you want now, has a lot to do with your ability to extend yourself and your mark in the world. However, are we ready to mother our futures? Some of us are still trying to figure things out ourselves!

And while figuring things out on our own, we often make decisions that leave us feeling unsettled. I remember being fearful the Lord was making me pay for the things I'd done in the past, that I'd gone too far and messed up my future. I even became fearful for the friends who were around me, that they would be punished for what they or I had done. How many of us have been in this space of knowing there are some things we've done out of God's will, and being afraid that not much more would happen for us?

Worse, if we're dealing with condemnation more than conviction, it can then become a cycle of believing, "Well, I might as well do my thing anyway, since my future won't be better . . ." This is how the enemy would have us think. That there is nothing to look forward to since we've messed everything up. But that cycle changed for me when I began speaking against the lies and learning more about God's character. And now I can be confident in the fact that if God is merciful to forgive and if he is our Father, then surely he still wants us to experience what is beautiful. You still have the ability to birth what is great. You still have the ability to put out in the earth what God has predestined with the thought of you.

Don't rush it! Think things through. Otherwise, our

trying to make things happen on our own, and looking at those around us, can lead to clouded judgment. During the time I was outside God's will for me, for example, a few of my acquaintances seemed to be down to keep bringing children into the world with no long-term plan, while my married friends who had waited and did it God's way had miscarriages. After a while, I noticed that there didn't seem to be many consequences for some people around me. We began having more and more baby showers. And because I had consumed a certain way of life through media, I began to water down my standards and agree it was okay to step out of the familial structure God had designed. I was okay with embracing the world's new normal. Culture began conditioning me. I was losing my sense of accountability and individuality. I had to constantly tell myself, "Don't make rash or emotional decisions out of fear and to lock a man down." I say the same to you: take your time. Don't rush God because of the things you want to pursue. And never believe it's too late to change course if you make a mistake. This lesson from the Holy Spirit was a lesson not just for my future family but for me spiritually and physically in *everything* I wanted to accomplish. Talk to yourself when you need to. Again, don't feel like it's getting too late!

Get rid of anything that is dark or causes your mind to be clouded and affect your decisions. Get in tune with your mental state and do some self-discovering to see where you honestly are. I call these self-checks. Ask yourself, "What's driving this decision?" I've interpreted this as: get rid of anything that isn't coming to you from heaven. Release anything that causes you to be distracted from the honest message that your soul, and heart, carries, because that is your answer. That is your purpose. It could be the voice of God. For a long time, I'd disregard the uncomfortable feelings or intuitions that were "strong enough to save my soul." My soul was telling me to say less with certain people, do more with this, end that relationship, stop playing house, etc. These heart-sent messages were all nudges that have to do with my real purpose.

So while there are consequences we have to live with from our poor decisions, there are also ways to avoid them. We should ask ourselves, "Where is my heart? What is it saying?" When my heart isn't in good condition, I am not healthy enough to hear or take on what God is calling me to produce. I strongly believe the enemy has tried to interrupt our true flow of production—including our God-given ideas—because he knows the possibilities are divinely great. Instead he gives us false paths, like he did with Eve in the garden. Understanding that even the physical part of me is still connected to the spiritual side of me, the enemy will always be on the hunt. As long as I am oblivious to the warfare around and focused only on me, I'll miss the mark and live without any direction. If I am weak in the fight, I will be easily influenced and unable to tap into how I can create the best life and environment for what I bring forth into the world. And remember: Just because you've lived and acted one way doesn't mean you always have to.

Whatever your desire, I hope you can apply the same lessons to whatever you are eager to accomplish, looking to God for his timing and plan. And for those of you who have followed God's plan and are still struggling, I encourage you to know that God is a healer and he can give you a miracle. Sometimes we need to shift our prayers to know if it's his will for us to accomplish things in the way that we dream, or if he has a different way in mind.

_____prayer

*Lord, we are in a day when producing spiritually and naturally has been at war. But Father, I ask that you multiply in me the ability to birth something new. Please bless me. I trust you will grant me my desire if it is the right path for me. You would not allow me to be without, if it is your will. Father, prepare me to take on what you're ultimately calling me to. I come against miscarriages. If a miscarriage—be it of a child or an apparent loss of my dream—is a part of my story, help me to peacefully get through but help me to move forward. Help me not to worry about what I am called to produce. Prepare me for the seed you're planting in me, and strengthen me. And if I have not walked in your ways, Father, forgive me for my sins and sexual immorality. Have me to walk in freedom with no guilt, understanding that you are the God of forgiveness and not only of punishment. Anything that I am unable to produce, I trust that it isn't your will. Lord, walk with me and have me to see the good things that are happening around me. In Jesus's name I pray. Amen.*

Blessed are those who fear the Lord, who find great delight in his commands. Their children will be mighty in the land; the generation of the upright will be blessed. Wealth and riches are in their houses, and their righteousness endures forever.

PSALM 112:1–3

He will love you and bless you and increase your numbers. He will bless the fruit of your womb, the crops of your land—your grain, new wine and olive oil—the calves of your herds and the lambs of your flocks in the land he swore to your ancestors to give you.

DEUTERONOMY 7:13

"For my thoughts are not your thoughts, neither are your ways my ways," declares the Lord. "As the heavens are higher than the earth, so are my ways higher than your ways and my thoughts than your thoughts."

ISAIAH 55:8–9

# CHAPTER 14

# Stop Looking at the Other Woman (Because You've Got the Juice)

**O**ftentimes, I would compare myself to an ex's new girl-friend or to who they were cheating with. I realized I had begun building my confidence on a foundation of comparison to "the other woman." I thought because my ex chose her, there was something more I needed.

That foundation set me up to fail. It had me basing my worth on a woman who was attached to my disappointment (and who was likely still figuring out life themselves), and someone I simply didn't know. I also had to face the fact I was placing my validity in the hands of another human being.

Though it seemed like I had confidence during this period of my life, I was exploring a hard truth about myself in my personal time. I began to realize that what I had was a shallow confidence. There was no depth to it. At any moment, if someone said anything close to my insecurities, I was ready to defend and abort mission. I was sensitive, damaged, and on guard. The moment an ex dated someone I felt was on a different level, my confidence was shattered. I began thinking that because I was bigger than her, my "big" wasn't attractive after all. Until finally, I started saying to myself, "I am a tasty cup of tea, I just may not be HIS cup of tea. But it definitely doesn't take away from the heat I bring to the table or the fact I am what I am; and that is . . . a cup of tea." I began zoning in on the beautiful things about myself. I owned my truths about my insecurities and this new confidence I was beginning to experience. I owned my flaws and the most amazing parts of me. For instance, I have freckles under my eye that many have mistaken for running eyeliner. For a long time, I wanted to get them removed, but I changed my way of thinking and said, "Oh no, honey! That's what makes you, you!" I thought about my beautiful smaller friends, who had men lined up, and believed I had to be smaller to get some attention, but I then I redefined what the world called "fat" as "the juice," and my true confidence transformed the way others saw me as well. I also realized I had men lined up for me too! They just weren't always the men I wanted. But that also helped me realize my worth wasn't dependent on a man's attention anyway.

In the end, I saw that my insecurities had swallowed up the truth of my being an attractive young woman. I had been living in darkness and not in God's light and truth of who I really was. The enemy wanted me blind. He wanted me to think less of myself so I wouldn't say yes to what I actually deserved. My blindness caused me to settle and say yes to whatever came my way. And since I wasn't going to the Word like I should have, I was ready to believe the lies that entered my ears instead of the truth and affirmations God wanted to place in my heart.

Don't look to the other woman—or anything else—to determine your value. It's okay to be inspired by positive qualities, but *you* should define what style, grace, success, and beauty is in *your* world. Embrace who you are and develop your depth. At one point, I started studying the characteristics of the Proverbs 31 woman and took on my proud voice and said, "Yaaassss! Honey, I am baadddd." I had to celebrate myself and the work God was completing in me. I then had a conversation with one of my closest friends and showed her I had reached a place where I display all the characteristics. Now, this growth won't happen to you overnight and all by yourself, but it will happen in your relationship with God as you allow him to show you who you are. He created you as your own individual, and to top that, he even labeled you as one of his children, a special person close to him. We need to always honor the individuality God has granted us as a gift. Your day and way of seeing the world is completely unique and different from anyone else's in this world. Even the things you may not like about yourself, God makes them a part of your purpose. And since God is the God of all, and all-knowing, he knows firsthand that you are beautiful. Inside and out. Our souls become even more beautiful when we spend time with him, and the person we grow into becomes more attractive to others after accepting what *he* values.

Learn and know who you are. You are beautiful. No other woman, man, or culture defines who you are. Remember, you'll be who you are with or without them. Own that!

_____**prayer**

*Father, help me to become so secure within myself that I am not curious of what's going on next to me. Assist me in believing you are doing something so great in my world, I have no concerns with anyone's business that doesn't call for me. And overall, come alongside so I can walk in peace, grace, and confidence. Remove any memories of damaging words that were spoken to my being and who I am. Help me heal from what others thought I should do and be, with the idea they'd make me better in their sight, and the temptation to look the way they think I should. Remind me of my value. Since I am the apple of your eye, I will be appreciated as an apple in someone else's eyes. And also remind me that what others think does not determine my existence on the earth. Father, supply me with relationships and connections that allow me to see the beauty from within. Surround me with people who have heaven-bound mindsets, so that they are in tune with you, speaking nothing but truth into my spirit, my subconscious. You think I'm so valuable that I should know I'm in a class all by myself. Help me to realize that there is no comparison. I'd like to be unmoved by the opinions of people and validated by heaven. I love you. And I love what you've done with me. Amen.*

## scriptures to consider

We do not dare to classify or compare ourselves with some who commend themselves. When they measure themselves by themselves and compare themselves with themselves, they are not wise.

**2 CORINTHIANS 10:12**

The Lord is faithful, and he will strengthen you and protect you from the evil one.

**2 THESSALONIANS 3:3**

Peace I leave with you; my peace I give you. I do not give to you as the world gives. Do not let your hearts be troubled and do not be afraid.

**JOHN 14:27**

# CHAPTER 15

# Never Mind. I'm Redefining It!

We all strive to be the best version of ourselves we can be. And in the process, we sometimes put pressure on ourselves to be "better" by watching everyone else on social media, in our lives, within our career, etc. Think about it: you can always find a master class, an article on how to be the greatest designer, information on how to become a millionaire in five seconds, a book on how to lose weight in ten days, or advice on "what it means to be successful." So many are searching for answers and are desperately working hard for the next big thing, but are unclear if it's *their* next big thing. We often compare ourselves and let the world tell us what we need to be and do. We'll even be convinced that our purpose is something other than what we initially thought after having gone through life and feeling like it's taking forever to get where we wanted to be.

As I said in the last chapter, I've come to grips with the fact that just because someone else is called beautiful, that doesn't make me unbeautiful. It means we are both beautiful, just in different ways. And it applies to more than appearance. Someone else's success doesn't take away from my success unless I let it. I get inspiration from Oprah and Gayle's relationship, how they are both powerful women but they're not defeated by who is greater. Each person on this earth is great in their own right.

When thinking of a chair, what are the legs to the chair without the seat on top of the legs? Everyone has a purpose. Both the legs and the seat are necessary to make the chair a successful/useful piece. How petty would it be for the legs of the chair to think that the seat is of greater substance all because it sits on top of the legs? I mean, just think of the legs saying, "I'd rather be up there than holding all of this weight of both the seat and the person." With a mindset like that, the legs of the chair wouldn't see the beauty of its strength and how powerful their purpose is. It's senseless. If both aren't there to fulfill their purpose, no one can comfortably sit. The point is, there's room for everyone.

Comparing ourselves to the next person only steals our joy, causes us to lose focus and creativity, and creates jealousy. We'll never come out ahead in a mental competition with someone else, especially because that someone is likely not giving a flying pig about you, or may be miserable because of their own comparisons to others. Why should you make yourself miserable or spend your time focusing on them?

Whose life are you trying to live instead of your own? What does success mean to you? I can say that what I wished to have five years ago, I now wonder, "Why was I even praying for that?" At just the thought, I am frowning and looking confused as if I wasn't that person. My goal for success at one point was only to have money! I mean, having a good stream of income is still a part of the goal, but now my focus is to be successful by being thorough in my business dealings, being healthy, being a good friend, being heaven-bound, remaining a solid daughter, sister, and friend, and being a good person to myself inside and out. All because I started looking at everything I needed, not only what the world taught me to think I needed.

Don't get me wrong; I'm not saying don't have inspirations, goals, and ambitions based on examples you see around you. I'm not saying become complacent with mediocrity. I am saying love yourself enough to not mute yourself by being so busy comparing yourself to what the next person is doing. Set realistic goals for yourself, stay in God's face, and ask him, "What's next for me? And how can you help me get there in my own way?" You were brought into the earth with a purpose, and the only thing that should be driving you is the reason you are here. What's that purpose?

Define what you call success by whether or not you're slaying your life assignment. Ask God, "Am I making you smile?" Living becomes easier when you're in your lane. You were designed to deliver! God gave you equipment for the days you've not even seen. Redefine it, sis!

_____**prayer**

*Father, remind me who I am in you. Open the eyes of my heart so I can see success is not determined by culture, and that trends change and people are fickle. Help me keep my anchor in you and in your Word. I thank you for showing me what I am to do in this world so I am not tossed to and fro, working hard for something I was never called to chase instead of going after what I need. I ask that you show me what success looks like, and that I become content with what I am supposed to have. Help me reach the goals that are for me to reach, and give me the strength and tenacity to push harder on those things. I trust you are with me and helping me find clarity in who I am. Forgive me for missing what you have been doing in my life while I was off looking at everyone else. Don't allow me to present a false profile to the world, and help me own what I have to offer to the world. I come against the voids of trying to measure up. I trust that you're with me and constantly filling me up with your love and overflowing truth. Make me secure with the new level of fulfillment this greater connection with you gives, and the intimacy you allow me to share with the great people I have in my life. Amen.*

Each one should test their own actions. Then they can take pride in themselves alone, without comparing themselves to someone else, for each one should carry their own load.

GALATIANS 6:4–5

Oh, don't worry; we wouldn't dare say that we are as wonderful as these other men who tell you how important they are! But they are only comparing themselves with each other, using themselves as the standard of measurement. How ignorant!

2 CORINTHIANS 10:12 (NLT)

For we are God's handiwork, created in Christ Jesus to do good works, which God prepared in advance for us to do.

EPHESIANS 2:10

# CHAPTER 16

# Chill Out!

Very often, we are more concerned with building our accomplishments than we are with building our bodies. During one of my SistHER mentorship video conferences, I had my doctor and friend, Dr. Dejarra Sims, as a guest. I asked her if there was a difference between the generations and how we care for ourselves. She said, "The generations of women aren't taking care of their bodies as they are taking care of their brands." We discussed other topics within the mentorship and somehow we traveled, in conversation, to how our bodies nurture a baby, our minds, and our purpose. She said as an example, "Babies are like parasites. They need the proper nutrients and rest to grow." What became clear is that if you aren't taking care of yourself, you won't be able to successfully fulfill your purpose.

The Lord dealt with me and had me to realize that what happens in the natural happens in the spiritual. Just like babies are "parasites," our businesses, marriages, friendships, children, schooling, etc., all depend on us—the condition we are in. If we never take time to chill and relax, we no longer have the potential to thrive. We're no longer on top of things mentally, so we can't get our dreams together and keep them going, or have the physical strength and capabilities to power through what's ahead.

For a while, I thought that being a part of the "no sleep gang" was the thing to do. I thought that being up late and having early mornings showed a different level of commitment and sacrifice. Don't get me wrong, sometimes I work late. However, my behavior began disrupting my restorative process, which contributed to me not always operating fluently in my assignment, in my gift, or in my purpose. When it came time for me to sing, my performances weren't what I knew they could have been because I hadn't rested well. I left a performance wondering if they'd have me back, since I wasn't at my best thanks to a lack of sleep. When I don't rest, I also get snappy and my mind isn't clear. I've had to do a lot of apologizing to my close friends and family simply because I was tired. Sometimes I'll get overly emotional and forget a lot of what I need to remember. Plus, God deals with me in my sleep when it comes to my clothing line, Eleven60, and my personal life. In my dreams, he shows me designs, situations I'll face, and people I should pray about. So when I don't rest, not only does it affect how I operate in purpose, it cuts down a line of communication between God and me. Hence, if I don't sleep, I won't dream, and I won't get the blessings I could have. God has a dream for you to dream, and it may be the answer you have been looking for.

God rested on the seventh day. What makes us think we shouldn't? Sister, you must rest. If your responsibilities are keeping you awake, do a workout to release some of that stress. I've noticed that when I get a good workout in, I sleep like a log. I know it may seem like we are working harder than ever, but remember you are a woman of God and you must maintain your grace. So prioritize and make sure you have two slots a day for yourself. What for? To sleep and to breathe. And it's really okay to say no to things in order to get that precious time. I've been finding joy by sometimes sitting in the car. No music. I put the phone down and just inhale and exhale.

Sometimes your no or your unavailability will even save your life, restoring your body and mind. Treat your time like your money. If you don't know how to spend your money, people will spend it for you. Spend your time on yourself, and rest.

Also be careful of what you enter into without knowing what it will require of you. I've noticed my mother's confidence and how she handles life. She's not moved by much and she underpromises. If I ask my father for something, he'll give one of two answers. It will be a for-sure yes or

"We'll see . . ." That is him saying, "I'd love to do this for you but, on this one, I am not making any promises." Sometimes underpromising is the way to life. That doesn't mean you don't have standards or commit to things, but I am saying consider it all so that you aren't exhausting yourself because of saying yes too soon. When you're having a hard time saying no, weigh it out. Protecting your time and mental state is its own kind of rest and care.

_____**prayer**

*Father, help me embrace rest. You were so concerned about me getting rest that you reserved one whole day for it. Forgive me for ignoring that part. Help me understand that rest is necessary for me to operate with purpose. Forgive me for overwhelming myself with more than I can handle. Remove the guilt or the idea I need to work with no end. The dream, the opportunity, the job is mine. Help me trust and believe that if I work for you, you will allow me to have it. But you would not allow me to work myself until I am no good. Your desire for me is to be good, to have good, and to feel good. While the world may seem to always be on a girl and picking up speed, help me to rest in your peace. Remove the frazzled feeling that causes anxiety or nervousness when it comes to my feeling like I need to keep up with an impossible standard. Eloi, please help me to slow down. Help me to trust your timing. Help me to sleep well so I can dream well. As I seek your will, it is well with my soul. Amen.*

## scriptures to consider

Remember to observe the Sabbath day by keep-ing it holy. You have six days each week for your ordinary work, but the seventh day is a Sabbath day of rest dedicated to the Lord your God.

EXODUS 20:8–10 (NLT)

The Lord replied, "My Presence shall go with you, and I will give you rest."

EXODUS 33:14

Come to me, all of you who are tired from carrying heavy loads, and I will give you rest.

MATTHEW 11:28 (GNT)

# Mind, Body, and Spirit

I n addition to rest, taking care of your total body is necessary to accomplish the things before you. When you feel healthy instead of weighed down, or mentally free instead of anxious, it sets you up to take on anything, because you know you're up for the task.

One thing that I've learned is that when I eat better, I sleep better and I think better. When I have my workouts, I tend to release frustration. (To be honest, I strongly dislike working out, but if I dance, I'm all into it.) And when my brain is free and my body is engaged, it places me in a better space to deal with everything in my personal life and business life after I'm done.

Maybe you're used to always having to pull it together or even keep it together, and you feel like every little thing falls on you. Find a way to worship the Lord by being active, because we were designed to be of body and of mind (the spirit) while in this world—the two work together. Taking time to care for the physical part of ourselves is caring for the entire temple God gifted to us on earth. And focusing on the body can sharpen the mind, giving it a chance to process everything smoothly. How often have you taken a walk or finished a shower, and a solution you were struggling over suddenly comes to you? Just like an arm moves smoothly without us having to control every nerve, our entire beings work best when we allow each part the ability and time to function naturally, and in balance.

I often get butterflies in my stomach when my spirit isn't settled or when I am taking on too much. The Holy Spirit will give you a nudge when you need to stop and focus on another part of your overall self. Don't ignore it, because the more we ignore it, the more we have a tendency to get overloaded.

# CHAPTER 17

# A Good Man

A lot of my early dating life was centered on the idea of finding a relationship and locking it down. The idea came from not wanting to be alone and seeing the love between my parents and others. I was infatuated with the idea of love and what it's supposed to look like with someone else.

I was in love throughout middle school, high school, and college. After having been through enough heartache during those years, and gaining respect for myself, I did everything I could to move on. As I mentioned earlier, I was engaged once before, but I realized I wasn't ready at that point. I kept getting the kind of nerves I didn't want to have while planning to enter marriage. It was because I wasn't comfortable at the thought of spending my life with someone else just yet. And as time went on and the wedding got closer, I realized I had said yes to the first man who had treated me well. I hadn't given myself a chance to experience more *gentlemen* while dating. This may sound ridiculous, but I was more in love with how he treated me and the idea of love itself. Therefore, I had an *idea* of the kind of man I wanted but because I had become so used to dysfunction, I immediately said yes to any signs of normalcy. Unfortunately, anything that was the total opposite of what I had experienced previously was considered normal for me. I was progressing, but I was still experiencing some forms of disfunction in my views of love. Hence, I was making premature decisions on life companionship. This wasn't healthy. In a sense, I was still operating with spiritual blindness. Clarity wasn't in my view.

After taking time to enjoy my single life, and getting to know myself and what I really wanted in not only a man but a life partner, my definition of love and what it means to be loved changed. And when I least expected it, God sent me my perfect man. My soon-to-be husband's self-discipline and self-control shined a light on some things I needed to fix about myself spiritually. He was loving my soul and didn't know it. He wasn't anxious to have a physical relationship with me. Instead he grabbed me tight and prayed for me.

The most beautiful thing is having a man who can make you feel like art. Make you feel like a woman. His grown-man characteristics and godliness cause me to feel safe so that I can maintain my grace. He tells me I'm beautiful, and

I know it's not only about my looks. When I am troubled, he'll grab my arm and tell me not to run from him, but to run to him. When I roll my eyes, he has no problem with it. With him, I don't have those nervous butterflies, but instead the kind that come from excitement and a surety I've never had before.

While we've been dating, we've been testing each other's hearts, and honoring the Lord in keeping ourselves until marriage. As you know, I have some bad habits and a big personality, but the beautiful thing is that he chooses to love me, all of me—my past, my now, and who I am becoming. And unlike some of my past relationships, he's helping me correct the way I've learned to protect myself. When I've said "I am done" in anger and fear, he'll tell me that we may argue and yell, but it won't be the end of us. There were times I'd ask him to leave, knowing I'd dread his departure, but he'd tell me, "I'm not going anywhere." The way God loves me through this man has caused me to embrace my Big on a whole other level. Sometimes I look at myself in the mirror, seeing things I once thought were ugly as beautiful. I am a force to be reckoned with because of this good man and good companionship.

All of that shows me exactly the type of love I was always looking for. I started thinking there weren't any good men out there but my daddy and grandfather, but like them Jordan is God-fearing, frugal, fun, protective, a good listener, and so much more. The God-like moments from him turn me on more than anything ever has in a man.

I want to connect myself with this man forever because he's not only loving me the way I deserve, he's healing me and making me who I've always strived to be. His words and his actions are healing the wounds I thought could never be completely taken away. I feel like the female Solomon right now because of how I'm writing about this love! I didn't think he was out there and now here he is, always wanting to protect me.

God has shown me it's possible to be loved the way I want to be loved. It's not so complicated after all. It's only complicated when we're with someone who doesn't have that love to give. And I've learned why it's important to do it God's way. When we try to make things work and hold on because of an idea of love we have in mind, it's hard to listen to God's will, and when we break away when the season is up, we are practicing a divorce. But when we are pursuing a relationship in its time, letting it unfold so we know that other person on a deep and spiritual level and are not forcing a connection, it transforms everything. I've been able to hear the voice of God so clearly. The Lord corrected me when I said, "It's too good to be true." Because he said, "Whatever I give you, it is GOOD and TRUE." He also had me adjust my thinking because I kept treating my "good thing" as if it weren't true. I didn't dwell with that person as if they were here to stay. Maybe you've been disappointed like me, needing to rid yourself of your former ways of thinking in order to enjoy the love the right person can give. Boy oh boy! It is true a good man can surely take you on a journey with the Lord.

I don't know what your perfect man will have, but God does. And the more we focus on the things God values and look for the type of love he lays out in his Word, the more our idea of perfection and his will intersect. Because if we go out looking for the wrong qualities, or try to push something before it's time, it's never going to work.

_____**prayer**

*Father, for so long, I didn't think having a true, deep, and equal relationship was possible. Forgive me for once upon a time being okay with this world's way of life and confusing physical connection and simply being treated well for love. I pray that you will help me grow so that I am ready for the relationship and the man you have chosen for me, someone who values respect, partnership, and you above all. Someone who is ready and willing to love me as you know I deserve to be loved—even if I don't know what that kind of love is yet. Continue to allow me to attract kingdom-like relationships so that we are in spiritual unity. And continue to prepare me for this life partner, if it's in your will. Help me to become the woman who will nurture the relationship through support, respect, grace, modesty, security, honesty, and wisdom. Amen.*

And now these three remain: faith, hope and love. But the greatest of these is love.

1 CORINTHIANS 13:13

Trust in the Lord with all your heart and lean not on your own understanding; in all your ways submit to him, and he will make your paths straight.

PROVERBS 3:5–6

Every good gift and every perfect present comes from heaven; it comes down from God, the Creator of the heavenly lights, who does not change or cause darkness by turning.

JAMES 1:17 (GNT)

# CHAPTER 18

# Gimme My Money

I remember being annoyed when family and friends would call me young, as if I still had a lot to learn. Now I wonder why I didn't consider even half of what they were advising me to do with my money.

My father and grandfather always encouraged me to save my money at a young age. Daddy began training my brother Drew and me when we were in middle school on how to manage our money by giving us a weekly allowance. If we went to him before the following week asking for money, he'd ask, "Where is *your* money?" If it was gone, that was it! No more spending. He gave us a budget to work with and if we didn't manage it well, we were broke. Drew's allowance was left for him in his room and mine was left in Daddy's office cabinet. I went by my parents' house the other day and went to get some envelopes, and an array of memories ran through my mind. I said to my father, "Daddy, this is where you used to put my allowance . . ." He laughed and I thought, there are definitely some things that I would have done differently with my money back then.

One thing I instantly remembered is that Drew had no problem acting as if he didn't have the money. He'd ask me to buy him food or ask Mommy to buy him clothes. For some reason, I never did what Daddy did, asking Drew where his money was. I would easily give it because he was my brother. Hilariously, and over the years, J. Drew saved up hundreds of dollars and was able to buy big equipment for his homemade studio and more.

The lesson is to sometimes act like you don't have the cash. (And by that, I don't mean always begging off your siblings or friends, ha!) Because if you tell yourself it's not worth spending *your* cash on, that cash stays in your pocket for more worthy expenses. This is a lesson the young me especially wishes she'd listened to. I could now say that, over the years, my father gave us enough money to invest so we'd be in good financial shape by the first year of college. In addition to my work and my career, which began when I was fifteen years old, over a million dollars came through my hands at a very young age. I say this not to brag—I know I've had some privileges not everyone has— but to help us consider the things God has given us that we have taken for granted. How many monetary gifts could we have saved so we'd have a small fortune or be able to take on the things we desire now? Let's even think beyond the idea of money. Maybe you had a special amount of audacity, strength, maturity, and strong relationships at a young age. Maybe you were surrounded by people who believed in you, but you never asked them to help you invest in growing those gifts. Or maybe you had someone who did invest in you, but you took it for granted. The only way for us to grow is to consider our ways, see the lesson in our past behaviors, and not repeat the same mistakes.

As a result of looking back on my past, I have been intentional in everything I do now. Sometimes I may buy some things that I want and don't need, but I have literally been praying a lot more about what I'm spending.

I used to be uninterested in the word *budget.* However, I have learned that if I don't set a budget, I will spend my whole paycheck and be left with nothing but stress and regret. (The same goes for spending time and talents—you can budget those too so you're able to do the bigger things you want to accomplish.) Don't be afraid of the word *budget.* After creating my budget, and always keeping in mind needing to save some for the future, I've easily been able to take care of the mortgage, light bills, car bill, and more. And because every cent I make was given to me by God, I am always able to give back to God the percentage he is due. He gave me talents and put dreams in me that led to streams of income beyond my music. It is all coming from the Lord. Before I started budgeting, I would sometimes panic or think about keeping that 10 percent back—but now I always have that 10 percent for him, because he is my number one budget item.

One thing I remember my grandfather saying is, "Just because you have it, doesn't mean you have to spend it." For the last several years, I've began putting the money in a savings account that is not for spending, and if ever I have something that I see and want, I consider my ways and what I already have, then say, "You don't have it, girl!"

I encourage you to look at your money and where it's going—because having the peace of mind that comes with wise spending is a whole lot better investment than any car or bag.

**prayer**

*Father, help me to be frugal with the income you provide. I dedicate even my finances to you. I give you full permission, and I submit to your authority, to come into my life and advise me on every moment of spending. Help me tell my dollars where to go. Don't allow me to be hesitant with saying no when I should not spend. Transform my way of thinking, transform my desires so that they match your will. I speak financial freedom over my life. I understand that with my faith, and with this declaration, there must be action. You are pushing me to be a woman of ownership in every part of my life. Be my advisor, and connect me with wise counsel. I also understand that how I manage my finances is an act of worship. I surrender even this part of my life to you. I have more than enough. I am blessed to be a blessing to others. Amen.*

Honor the Lord with your wealth and with the firstfruits of all your produce; then your barns will be filled with plenty, and your vats will be bursting with wine.

PROVERBS 3:9–10 (ESV)

Whoever can be trusted with very little can also be trusted with much, and whoever is dishonest with very little will also be dishonest with much. So if you have not been trustworthy in handling worldly wealth, who will trust you with true riches?

LUKE 16:10–11

# CHAPTER 19

# Splurge . . . a Little

I know we just talked about the blessings of saving, but if you work hard and are responsible with your money, it is totally fine to treat yourself to something that is worth the expense every once in a while. A lot of women think we have to wait on others to show us the world. You don't, as long as you splurge on the things that matter. And sister, you matter.

I know spending money wisely on yourself can be a struggle—be it knowing where to spend it, or being willing to spend it at all. I found that because I became so particular about where every dollar went once I started budgeting, there were times I felt bad for treating myself. Especially as I like the finer things. After I made the purchase, especially if it was a trip or an experience, I would feel guilty because I felt the money could have been spent on something other than me. As a result, I had to tell myself, "You work hard and this purchase will be beneficial in the long run. Everything doesn't have to go in the vault." As long as I could afford it and my business planning was tight, spending a little to benefit myself in a big way was the best thing I could do with that cash.

How will you enjoy what you've earned? Tell your dollars where to go, but tell them to reward you when needed. If you have wanted the bag, the trip, the new bracelet, etc., and have thought it through, then go for it! And we should not feel the need to have it all at once. However, not all splurges are material. Sometimes, the splurge can be contributing something toward building your big dream rather than going out to eat or buying a piece from your favorite designer. Or a splurge could be less about putting the money out and more about focusing a little extra on a part of our lives than we normally would for the month or for the week. I remember choosing to splurge on what I was placing in my savings account, and I was overjoyed to see how much that extra money each deposit had grown my savings as a result. I was in a pleasurable mental space.

And those good feelings are needed in our lives. Once I began studying the mind and why it's important for us to be in good space mentally and emotionally, I learned about the chemical dopamine. Dopamine is important as a pleasure chemical in your brain that can make you feel rewarded, and a good level helps keep you healthy mentally and physically. Once I made it a priority to get a good balance of the chemical dopamine as a part of my brain activity, I felt more motivated. And seeing my emotional progress, my emergency fund growth, or potential real estate investments grow caused me to experience that pleasure chemical. Or even when I went to the five-star hotels, sat out at the pool with my big thighs out and no concern about what others thought, I felt good in the moment. These splurging moments were beneficial for my mental state and confidence. I was restored and even motivated to get back to work after a needed splurge.

Sometimes the splurge is necessary, sis. Splurge a little.

_____**prayer**

*Father, show me how to be wise with my spending habits, and how to know when to spend and when not to spend. Since you're this God who is in my now and my future, help me prepare for the things I don't see, and also help me to make the investment in myself with a little splurge, alongside your counsel. Thank you for my income and the opportunity to see the world and your glory. Help me to not be impulsive, but to be thorough while rewarding myself. Change my heart, whether it's too centered on the needs of others that I forget about myself or too focused on spending on trends that will pass and won't give me lasting pleasure. Help me to think my splurges through with an eye toward the future. Train me with my finances so that I can work smarter and not harder. Release in me great wisdom and strategies on financial literacy.*

*When I'm treating myself, or splurging, help me to experience your glory and your presence. Help me not to feel bad about treating myself, but own it! I own the fact that you are my God and you have provided these pleasurable experiences for me while here on earth. In Jesus's name, amen.*

## scriptures to consider

She considers a field and buys it; with the fruit of her hands she plants a vineyard.

**PROVERBS 31:16 (ESV)**

This is what I have observed to be good: that it is appropriate for a person to eat, to drink and to find satisfaction in their toilsome labor under the sun during the few days of life God has given them—for this is their lot. Moreover, when God gives someone wealth and possessions, and the ability to enjoy them, to accept their lot and be happy in their toil—this is a gift of God. They seldom reflect on the days of their life, because God keeps them occupied with gladness of heart.

**ECCLESIASTES 5:18–20**

# Six Ways to Secure the Bag

Some of us are posting the good life on social media while crying broke behind the screens and filters. Set some money aside so that you can see the world and enjoy the fruits of your labor. You work hard; you should play hard too. Or maybe you'd like to start a business, buy a home, or have another dream. You must secure the bag in order to take those steps. Truth be told, financial stability often allows us to be at peace mentally and physically. Secure the bag so that maybe you can get away!

## 1. Pay Yourself (Ecclesiastes 5:18–20)

Commit to paying yourself every week. Start an account that you will not withdraw from, and pay this account like it's rent or a mortgage. Don't touch the money once it's deposited. It can be as small as ten to twenty dollars per week or per month! Whatever you can afford, though as we all know, the bigger, the better.

We should all have an emergency fund. Do you have one? If your answer is no, then you should start an account today and try this method! Thank me later.

## 2. Play Broke & Learn to Say No (Psalm 128:2)

While I was single, I gracefully accepted the title of being a single woman. I didn't have a lot of extra because I was all by myself, honey! I needed every pinch of change. Similarly, just because you have it, that doesn't mean you have to spend it. It's okay to turn down something because it's not where you want to put your cash. And just because you have it for *yourself* doesn't mean you have it for everyone else.

Similarly, if someone wants to treat you, accept the offer. Learn to accept the blessings. Don't be "leechy," but accept the generosity. A large percentage of Americans use about 40–60 percent of their income on eating out. I once told my mentees, "If you really wanna go out but don't have a lot of cash, grab a saucer and just ask everybody at the table if you can taste what they have." You will have had a full entree with no bill!

## 3. Cash Envelope System

Leave the credit cards at the crib! Leave the debit card too. Give yourself a daily (or monthly) budget and only have it in cash! I repeat, only have it in cash! Once you have no more cash in your envelope, you're done. That's it. Take yo' tail back home, rest your feet, and eat some chips. Act like a college student.

This also helps you become more aware of what you're spending your money on—and helps you save for the things you really want, which then helps wire your brain for budgeting overall.

## 4. Invest (Ecclesiastes 11:2)

Invest in a mutual fund or a certificate of deposit (CD). Find ways to grow your money other than at your local bank—like in real estate or in stocks. When we see we can earn higher interest on our money, we also find a better way of living.

## 5. Adapt a New Mentality. Leave a Legacy! (Proverbs 13:22)

Age has nothing to do with this. Whether you're fifteen or forty-five, if you want to start up a business, these tips are for you. A lot of young people have vision and don't know where to start. I've seen so many young people with a great gift, and it goes toward the streets because they didn't know where to start with their ability to flip things and save money. Don't run through money like water—use it responsibly, with your future in mind. And don't ever be okay with growing a life where you always have to worry about money. Evaluate how well you've managed your income—what you spend it on, how much you have left after paying the necessities, what you are able to save, etc. And pay people back. Don't keep digging holes in your future because you owe people money. You already have bills to pay, and so do they (Romans 13:8, Proverbs 22:26–27)!

And look at life insurance. God forbid, but if

something happens, it will let your loved ones grieve properly without having to start a GoFundMe account to cover any expenses. And if you choose the right plan, it can work as an investment for you as well.

### 6. Honor God with What You Have (Luke 18:12)

Last but not least, honor God with your increase (Proverbs 3:9). Sometimes we feel like we have a hole in our pocket because we aren't honest with our money (Malachi 3:8–10). We don't give God his tenth. So he makes sure he's securing his bag too, LOL. In what ways are we investing it back into the kingdom or honoring God with what he has given us? I'm a cheerful giver and so I give to others. I give to my home church and other ministries that have blessed me in order to advance the kingdom and in hopes of extending their reach. I pay my tithe, and I've never cried broke, in addition to being a good manager of my money.

# CHAPTER 20

# I'm Not a Businessman, I'm a BUSINESS, Man!

This line is from one of my favorite rappers, Jay-Z. What I love is that is shows everything you do matters. You are a walking billboard for your personal "brand." And because of how the world works, some resources and opportunities are dependent upon how you carry yourself.

When I was younger, my father kept telling me things like, "Those are house shoes." I would then say, "These aren't house shoes" or "This is the trend." He always put his foot down when it came to what I had on in public. For example, I had to be sneaky to wear those shoes to school (which I did). I also remember one time after we'd moved to a bigger home, I left the house with a head wrap on and some sweats. He asked me, "Kierra, where are you going?" I was headed to the mall. He then began counseling me on my mentality and ways of thinking, because I had also started becoming far more comfortable with wearing that same kind of attire whenever I was flying out for work. He said, "Not only are you a representation of me, but most of all yourself. If you were a walking billboard, what would people read?"

If I was a hairdresser, and I didn't have a business card on me at the time, my hair could possibly be a marketing tool for my business. If I'm a curvy woman (which I am), and I'm owning my apparel, and saying I am a designer, how I look could attract compliments, no attention at all, or even a negative impression; my appearance is the first conversation with a potential client. Even how you carry yourself overall makes a difference. Unfortunately, there are many times when people will profile or stereotype you based on their own broken selves—and that is an entirely different battle—but there are also perceptions you *can* control and use to present your best self. Because what I've learned is that you—every part of you—are the first representation of your brand, your soul, your God, and your business. And if you honestly present yourself as a reflection of those inner beauties, it could change others' perceptions as well, and possibly help them reflect on themselves.

My father became an example to me of that kind of

I'm Not a Businessman, I'm a BUSINESS, Man!

reflecting. I've watched how he handles his business. It isn't just his profession; it includes his family, his faith, his health, his home, and more. He is a walking advertisement for himself that shows punctuality, aspirations, goals, faith, love, and organization. He doesn't play with his time. And his car always looks like it was just driven from the carwash and detailed. The inside and the outside are always clean. He didn't let us eat in the car when we were younger. We would sneak fries, and he would catch us in the rearview mirror. He values cleanliness. We would laugh hysterically at the time, but I've realized he was teaching us that you set the rules for how you are to be treated: If you treat yourself and the things you value as valuable, others will treat you as valuable. And if you don't treat yourself with great value, you show others how they can treat you.

And while watching my father, I've ultimately learned that we as kingdom citizens show the world what we value as God's ambassadors. Hence, my life must be about me being on my business. Being on my square! Allowing room for human error but never falling too far out of my position. Staying alert and ready for war or the next God opportunity. Reading and learning new ways of shining in the world so that I am a timeless individual. A legacy that will speak when I am no longer here. And this mindset of Christ's is something we as God's people need to develop if we are to shine well—because if our light is dim or not advertising the things we value, our billboard can turn people off from us and what we are trying to display. For example, while growing up in the church, I always wondered why some of the most devoted people's children refused to believe in God. The answer I came up with was that the devoted people around them made this Jesus thing look boring or time consuming, with no visible benefit. Sometimes we are the "Jesus" people meet for the first time. What does Jesus look like on you?

I've tried to apply that idea to my own life. Since emulating Jesus is the ultimate goal, one of the Scriptures that stuck out to me was him being about his Father's business. I noticed that whenever he asked his disciples, "Why are you looking for me?" it was almost as if Jesus was saying, "You already knew I would be on my square. On my business. Taking care of what is important. My business has to do with my purpose on the earth." Once my mentality changed, I learned that I'm not only a walking billboard for myself, I am a representation of who God says I am. I am a representation of him. Making sure my appearance is on point not only shows people I am together, it presents a good representation of what God is doing in my life. I can use my platform to spread his message honestly and openly, and treat everyone around me with respect. Doing anything and everything I can when it comes to dreaming or going for what is ultimately big.

I wanted to change my mentality because when I'm about my Father's business, I'm on course—not distracted or focusing on the things the devil tries to place in my way. Being about the Father's business for you can even entail living out the Scriptures to the best of your ability. Allowing God's Word to be like a checklist. I can tell you firsthand that when I started making my business God's business, I began seeing that God lays out literally everything in his Word. He talks about dating, mental stability, finances, marriage, our homes, our business, our children, and more. He left nothing out.

So what will your billboard say? And what will your business look like to the world?

_____prayer

*Father, help me to be about my business. Help me to be laser focused like Jesus. Anytime there was a suggestion from the enemy, such as what happened on the mountaintop with the devil, Jesus said, "Man shall not live by bread alone, but on every word that comes from the mouth of God." Make me so focused that I'm able to respond with your Word from my heart. Show me your words for me as well. Help me unlock the Scriptures so I can live them out. I am your business. I ask for, and accept, a promotion. Let the gospel shine through me. Most of all, help me to be a walking billboard of your love, your grace, your integrity, your faithfulness, tenacity, focus, creativeness, and your glory. Help me to walk in the beauty of your majesty. Amen.*

"Why were you searching for me?" he asked. "Didn't you know I had to be in my Father's house?"

**LUKE 2:49**

And observe what the Lord your God requires: Walk in obedience to him, and keep his decrees and commands, his laws and regulations, as written in the Law of Moses. Do this so that you may prosper in all you do and wherever you go.

**1 KINGS 2:3**

# CHAPTER 21

# Cheat Days

I was once over three hundred pounds. My nanna was always concerned about my health at that point because I was so young. And Nanna being Nanna, she wasn't afraid to tell me the truth when needed.

I tell this story all the time: The first thing you have to know is, Nanna always had good tea and good cookies. And the side door we always came in led straight into the kitchen. And how could anyone not look to see what their grandmother has to eat? One day I came in, using the key I had to her house, and she was still getting dressed. Once she was finished, she found me in the kitchen, eating. My eyes got big because I had recently mentioned to her the diet I was trying. She said, "Well, where is the diet?" I answered,

"Today is a cheat day!" She then responded, "You look like a cheat day. You don't need any more cheat days! Stick to it!" I laughed hysterically. Almost to the point of me wheezing while laughing. It was absolutely hilarious. I couldn't believe she called me a cheat day.

While we are in an era that causes many of us to be overly sensitive, finding the gem in this moment has changed my life forever. I never forgot it, especially as I've seen her words apply to my life beyond my weight. For instance, while we say we are believers and worshipers, it's so easy for us to say one thing but do another. My nanna's statement basically said, "Your actions aren't matching your words. It's showing up, heavily, in your life and even in your appearance." When we have an encounter with the Lord, it shows up in our attitude, the way we love, and in our very appearance. Exodus 34:29–30 says Moses came down from the mountain after meeting with God, and he was actually glowing so much people couldn't look at him for very long. Our lives and our bodies can also show the effects of God's presence. Or the lack of it.

I've been thinking about some friends who are the same age as me, but who look older because of the things they've decided to make a never-ending cheat day. It's almost like they had a war on the battlefield with life itself. When we participate in damaging habits, it very often shows by the discoloration of our lips, our eyes, and our hands, our mind-sets toward the world, and more. I often thought I could hide my sexual sins better than my other sins, but that showed up in my attitude. It showed up in my disposition. Spiritual evidence was showing up in my behaviors because I had too many cheat days—and with the wrong person.

This lesson forced me to come to grips with the fact worship is not just a song we sing or a cry that we add to it. It's a lifestyle. It challenged me to see that my weight was a sign of my lack of self-discipline. Honestly, I wanted to do something about it, and I wanted to be healthy. And once I stopped living a cheat day life, what I ate became part of my act of worship. It was a sign to God of how I appreciated the body he had given me. So much was in this lesson from my nanna.

What parts of your life have become cheat days? How can you give up those things to God as a sign of your commitment to him today?

_____**prayer**

*Father, I have tasted some things, and they've tasted good to my flesh but not to my spirit. I am asking that you allow me to have your supernatural strength, help, and self-discipline to conquer these challenges. I ask, God, that you come into my heart, into my mind, and into my very being, living through me. Make the choices through me. Help me to say no quickly and have the will to follow through. I ask that you deliver me. Let your will be done. Forgive me for days I've taken a break from our relationship. Please cleanse me from any unrighteousness. Change my taste buds and desires so I don't crave the things that* once tasted good to my flesh. Please don't let this be a struggle any longer. Help me to conquer it in my mind. The only way to win this battle is with your help, your presence in my life. You know the things that I need help with. I lay them at your feet. I give it to you. Where I am weak, you are strong. Please be my strength. I declare over my life that the cheat days will one day become a memory and no longer a habit. I have authority over it through Jesus Christ. I understand that it's not only the win that matters but it's also developmental process that contributes to my success. I won't get weary while on the journey. I will see it through. In Jesus's name I pray. Amen.

## scriptures to consider

Therefore, if anyone is in Christ, the new creation has come: The old has gone, the new is here!

**2 CORINTHIANS 5:17**

# Forget the Dumb Stuff

My nanna may have come off harsh to some with her blunt approach, but she loved God, and I was often blown away by her. She would serve others in a fast second. Give money if she had it on her right then and there. She loved giving and finding an answer for others. She wanted to see people win. She didn't care to be in the spotlight, but she wanted to do the work of the Lord. She was devoted to my grandfather and her family. Seeing my nanna and my grandfather together was so much fun to watch. He would make funny faces when he didn't agree with her, and she'd freely express her opinion back. We'd all laugh and carry on. She had three good friends, and I noticed that was because she was very selective with where she spent her time.

Her most-used phrase was, "Forget the dumb stuff!" I would share stories with her to get her perspective, and if it was a waste of time, she'd suggest the best thing to do was to disregard what was senseless or what wasn't worth my time. She challenged me to consider all things but to not live with, or accept, anything less-than. She wanted me to think high, like Philippians 4:8. She walked with her head high. I never saw my nanna with her head down.

I remember telling her about a guy I was dating, and she asked, "How long have y'all been dating?" I told her ten years. She responded, "Forget the dumb stuff." She later said, "Baby, that's a marriage. That's too much time." I laughed, trying to brush it off. She drove her point by saying, "Y'all might as well be married and miserable." I laughed even harder because I honestly wasn't happy. As we went on and talked about it, she reminded me to be mindful of what and who I give my time to. While it was hard to hear, she helped me see I didn't always have to hold on to something, especially if all it gave me was heartbreak and disappointment.

My nanna meant so much to me. I miss her and her wisdom every day.

# CHAPTER 22

# Save Something for Yourself

One of my best friends, Tamika, passed away to sickle cell anemia. She was one of the first people outside of my family to show me what sisterhood and true friendship was about. Through her, I learned that God does speak through friends, and that he loves on us through others. I miss her dearly, because she could always give me the advice I needed. Around the time when Instagram became popular, I began sharing so much of my life. I was anxious to post pictures. She asked me, "What will you have for yourself if you give everything to the public? Leave a little mystery." This helped me to develop what the Bible calls "discretion." (See the Proverbs 2:11 verse at the end of the chapter.)

When we use discretion, it keeps people from seeing

our "growing" moments, when we are still figuring life out, which disables them from holding our past over our heads in our future. When we do certain things, like posting every part of our lives, we add to our spiritual warfare. In other words, some negative things come into our lives because of what we release into the atmosphere. It's almost like we're handing the opponent a battle plan to use in the war against us. I remember posting a pic of one of my favorite artists and me at their concert. The religious people were so over the top because they felt I was endorsing a non-Christian lifestyle. I began defending myself for simply having a good time, but realized I put myself in a space that caused a need for explanations. Though posting that pic was the popular thing to do, it wasn't the best thing to do. As the Word says, "I have the right to do anything . . . but not everything is beneficial" (1 Corinthians 6:12). When using discretion, we give ourselves peace and room to figure things out apart from the spotlight. Or even keep personal memories for ourselves, moments not everyone needs to share in and comment on. I've noticed I sometimes get a bit possessive with my close family members and my friends. So I've begun cherishing and holding tight to videos and pictures of myself with loved ones. As much as I want to post and let the world see, at least I have something for myself. My personal business stays mine.

Because the truth is, the world doesn't need a view into all your business. Yes, social media is fun and the likes can be thrilling, and sharing juicy details with girlfriends can be fun, but giving too much of yourself away leaves you with little to hold on to that is really yours. Because once it's out in the world, the world is going to give their two cents. And for me mentally, saving some moments for myself is a part of owning my inner beauty, and owning and developing those internal things only I know about myself. I don't have to share every part of what is going on in my mind and in my life, and instead can think carefully about what I do make public.

During this journey, I've discovered that when you give too much of something so easily, it loses value. But when you take time to luxuriate in your life's riches for yourself, it can benefit you in so many ways. You get to know yourself and your thoughts, and can own your journey for yourself. You can learn from any lessons privately so you are enriched by the experience instead of cast down (or even unfairly judged) for your mistakes. And you get to hang on to the good that's around you, because those moments and experiences remain special and can be cherished.

_____prayer

*Father, help me to be okay with not giving the world, or culture, everything it asks for. When social media calls for my attention in so many ways, allow me to keep some moments for myself. Give me the strength and wisdom to choose what I want to give. Don't allow me to mask my problems, leaving me unable to deal with what's really going on in my life. Direct me in what I need to share, and with whom, from the good to the bad, so* that what I get back is fulfilling instead of draining. Father, I enjoy sharing love and generosity with others—help it remain enjoyable for me. Thank you that I can provide a blessing to someone else. However, direct me in ways to find a balance so I have some blessing left for me. You know the ways I'll need it most. So I surrender to you. Have your way in me and what I give to others. In Jesus's name, amen.

## scriptures to consider

Discretion will protect you, and understanding will guard you.

**PROVERBS 2:11**

Good sense is a fountain of life to him who has it.

**PROVERBS 16:22 (ESV)**

# CHAPTER 23

# Kill the Dragon

I had a song on my album *Graceland* called "Kill the Dragon." It's one of my favorites. A line in the first verse says, "He'll be there dressed for the fight, sword out and mouth full of lies . . ." What if I told you we were at war with this dragon that can fight and speak? The devil is the dragon. Now, what if we had at the forefront of our minds that he's determined to make sure there's nothing left of us? We'd be prepared to fight as if our lives depended on it. Unfortunately, it seems as though our culture, our new way of life, has watered down our level of spirituality and standards. Second Timothy 4:3 (ESV) says, "For the time is coming when people will not endure sound teaching, but having itching ears they will accumulate for themselves teachers to suit their own passions." We're often focused so much more on grace and forgiveness that we neglect love and commitment for God. We then become more concerned with what we want than what we need. Forgetting that we were all set here for a purpose, with a job to do. And the enemy uses that lost focus against us.

In addition, I've learned the enemy knows who we are and will not let up. He's aiming to completely devour us. He's not tiptoeing around with this. And usually when it's time to prepare for war, there's a lot of preparation. So how are we preparing? As a woman of faith, I have to keep in mind that I am of God. There's true opposition between me and the enemy (Genesis 3:15), and anything that is connected with me, the enemy wants destroyed. John 10:10 says, "The thief comes only to steal and kill and destroy." The enemy has a plan to take everything we have. And to be able to consider his way of thinking when it comes to the fight, I've had to keep in the forefront of my mind what it would be like if I were kicked out of heaven. I get nervous butterflies in my stomach at the very thought of it. I understand that because Lucifer was kicked out of heaven, he has some heavy jealousy toward me, and God's Word says that "jealousy is cruel as the grave" (Song of Solomon 8:6, KJV). Meaning it has no consideration for your life. Satan once had an opportunity to dwell in the same place as God. Imagine being so out of order that you no longer have God's grace on your life. And instead you are constantly seeing others experience God's faithfulness, peace, love, and favor. This would be the most disheartening thing ever.

However, again imagine being at war with the dragon.

Something huge, with natural instincts to kill and destroy. Though this culture says that we are progressing in ways of love, I've always asked myself, is this the kind of love God has ordained? Is God okay with this way of life? One of my biggest fears is missing the mark. Not just out of fear of going to hell but out of fear of missing God's love and presence. I despise any day where I don't hear him. With these things in mind, I began fighting for my soul. I believe there is a life after this one. Hence, I'm living as if I'm practicing for that life. As a result, I'm always considering that my battle is not with the flesh. Ephesians 6:12 says, "For our struggle is not against flesh and blood, but against the rulers, against the authorities, against the powers of this dark world." This Scripture informs me that my battle is more spiritual than it is physical. So, we must fight differently. This is a part of our ownership. Knowing the strategy in this battle. Owning the tools God has given us for this fight. He gives us a sense of discernment, not just as troopers but as commanders.

Knowing that our issue is not always with people but the spirit behind them causes us to use our time differently as well. This isn't just in our personal affairs, but in our business affairs. I've learned prayer is one of my weapons. Knowing God's Word is one of my weapons. In 2 Corinthians 11 alone, verse 3 speaks of his "cunning" ways, and verse 14 says that "Satan disguises himself as an angel of light" (ESV). First Peter 5:8 says that he's prowling and seeking like a lion to see who he can devour. Which is why I've been practicing more of what God's Word says.

The first battle with Satan on earth was with Eve, in the garden. From reading it, it seems clear he had the ability to walk and talk like humans. The curse was for him to move on his belly. If this is the case, then that same serpent is the one I have authority over. Luke 10:19 says, "I have given you authority to trample on snakes . . . nothing will harm you."

God's Word also says in 1 John 4:4, "The one who is in you is greater than the one who is in the world." This Scripture is one of those verses we often learn as children. And there's a reason we need to learn it when we're young, because these words let us know that we are built to win this war. The Scripture lets us know we can truly slay the dragon that is out to conquer our souls and lives. And that's why we shouldn't walk with fear or timidity.

Allow me to reassure you that though the enemy may tamper with our minds and though things may feel like they are right on the edge, you still have a chance to win! You're so powerful, you can come into a room with a whisper to declare what WILL happen in your life. Heaven is backing you up!! "Whatever you bind on earth will be bound in heaven, and whatever you loose on earth will be loosed in heaven" (Matthew 16:19). The terms *binding* and *loosing* comes from an ancient Jewish phrase, and means *to forbid by an indisputable authority* and *to permit by an indisputable authority*.[1] That

---

1. John Sutherland Black, Thomas Kelly Cheyne, *Encyclopaedia Biblica: A Critical Dictionary of the Literary, Political and Religious History, the Archaeology, Geography, and Natural History of the Bible, Volume 1,* "Binding and Loosing," (Adam and Charles Black, 1899), 573.

authority, through God, comes from within you. What makes the difference and unleashes that power is whether we actually believe the principles and ways of God's Word.

Kill the dragon! I mean, SLAY IT! Just like David did, confront the enemy with God on your side and with the power invested in you. Don't give the devil the authority to have a conversation but simply remove him immediately! Eve went wrong when she entertained the conversation. Don't let him sit with you. Don't let him sleep with you. Discern the spirit behind it, then move strategically, intentionally, and aggressively.

_____prayer

*Father, help me to fight this fight. Help me to win. I ask that you sharpen my discernment so I can move strategically as you would have me. Cleanse me from any unrighteousness so I am not distracted or prohibited from the given authority and power. Allow my relationship with you to show up when it's time for battle. Don't allow me to downplay what's real to me, as a believer, because of the relaxed approach culture has toward spiritual matters. Prepare me! Keep at the front of my mind that the world cannot understand all things. I come against every demonic force, I cover my life and my family's lives by speaking the blood of Jesus over us. I ask that you continue to equip me and show me that there is no age to this fight. I come against every lie. I will give no room for the enemy. He is defeated and cast out of all parts of my life. I will live and feed* off of your Word. Let your Word and power come alive in me, strong. I want to fight this fight with no fear, no confusion, no uncertainty. Make me clear of who I am in you—no spirit of darkness will silence me, nor blindfold me. I am free! I am a giant killer (1 Samuel 17:50, Matthew 1:1). It is in my inheritance. It's in the bloodline. Hence, I am a dragon slayer. By the power that is invested in me, I decree that no force of darkness will win. I am more than a conqueror and God is with me. In Jesus's name I pray. Amen.

## scriptures to consider

For we do not wrestle against flesh and blood, but against the rulers, against the authorities, against the cosmic powers over this present darkness, against the spiritual forces of evil in the heavenly places.

**EPHESIANS 6:12 (ESV)**

The thief comes only to steal and kill and destroy. I came that they may have life and have it abundantly.

**JOHN 10:10 (ESV)**

# CHAPTER 24

# Hearing God's Voice

The most uncomfortable thing is living a life and not knowing God's voice. I often say it's like an invention unclear of its purpose or operating with no communication with its inventor.

I touched on this a little in an earlier chapter, but when I started focusing more on God instead of bad habits and relationships, the results were amazing! As time went on, I was able to identify things I couldn't see before. I didn't have audible conversations with God, but his voice became clear to me and it became very obvious when he was showing me signs. Honestly, if I hadn't cut negative influences and behaviors out of my life, I wouldn't have been able to see when he was speaking to me through experiences, events, attitudes, conversations, etc.

The truth is, things that offend God cloud our mental space. We communicate with God spiritually, with our minds and our hearts. You have an unction in your soul. If God is a spirit and you're a soul, then there's a language that is understood on a deeper level. It's understood on an intangible level. And it's up to you to invest in that part of yourself to make sure the signals are clear and you're able to interpret. And making sure you have a clear path both ways to communicate is key.

God has even given me tangible examples of how important that type of communication is. I remember traveling to Japan as part of a tour for my sophomore record. While shopping there, I was talking louder, as if they couldn't hear me. It wasn't the volume that was the communication problem. It was that I didn't know any Japanese. Which is kind of like those moments with the Lord when we aren't in a good space with him—we're not speaking his language. As a result, we'll be asking him to show us a sign or we'll start to talk louder so he'll hear us, when instead we've been missing what he's been saying all along simply because we didn't take the time to understand and correct what we'd been doing wrong. While on the trip, I began paying closer attention to the phonetics in short phrases to see what accidentally offended them and what didn't. I then learned that many people there understood English if I wrote it down. This was working, but it took up a lot of time. I started getting tired of writing everything, until I realized that the people I was writing to were having to read and understand what I wrote, in my handwriting. We finally connected with each other because we decided to literally get on the same page, find a common language, and do the work. And let me tell you something: if we put in the work of getting on God's page and living in tune with the common language he put in our souls—understanding what he left us in Scripture and then living according to those words—God puts in work with us, meeting us more than halfway. When I put this into practice in my spiritual conversations, I became surer of when the Lord spoke to me because I was clear on how he speaks. He began answering me through sermons from my father, conversations with friends, Scriptures, and random occurrences that aligned with my spirit. Let's just say, God made sure he got the answer to me!

Nothing should take control of your life and cause you to lose your connection with the Lord. Instead, we should seek out relationships and situations that strengthen those connections and show us where we can grow. Seeing others' relationships with the Lord has highlighted the areas where I could strengthen mine. Get those channels clear, sis. Everything shouldn't be so fuzzy for you.

_____prayer

*Father, thank you for being so faithful and always ready to give me instruction on which way to go. Forgive me for consulting with so many other influences that have caused confusion. I've become so used to hearing everyone else's voice, including my* flesh, my fears, and more. But Father, now I ask that you come into my heart. Allow me to connect more deeply with you. I want to be clear when I hear your voice. I want to know when it's you pointing me in a certain direction. Convict me so that I'm uncomfortable when I'm out of your will. Don't allow me to be okay with what offends you, since things have become so widely accepted. Surround me with family and friends who are more concerned with my soul than they are my happiness. Don't allow me to lose my standard, which makes me different, royal. Cleanse me from any unrighteousness. Search my heart! If you find anything that shouldn't be there, take it out. While your grace may be sufficient, don't allow me to abuse it. In Jesus's name I pray, amen.

## scriptures to consider

Call to me and I will answer you, and will tell you great and hidden things that you have not known.

**JEREMIAH 33:3 (ESV)**

I will instruct you and teach you in the way you should go; I will counsel you with my loving eye upon you. Do not be like the horse or the mule, which have no understanding but must be controlled by bit and bridle or they will not come to you.

**PSALM 32:8–9**

# CHAPTER 25

# I'm Supposed to Be Here

**H**ave you ever questioned your very being? Wondered "What's my purpose?" Take a look at your gifts and talents. There's a plan for you, something big you might not even see for yourself! A place and a role you were born to fill.

At one point in my career, I was feeling empty, thinking singing was all there was to me. I wondered, what will happen when my time is up? I didn't want to be the hustling singer. I wanted God to sustain me. I didn't want to force myself in a space that wasn't right simply because I needed to find other work once my time in the big spotlight was up. I remember my mother saying to me around that time, "You don't have the gift of gab for nothing!" She later implied that public speaking was in my future. We laughed in the moment, but here she was, once again leading me to an answer without realizing how much I really needed it. And I listened: because of my love for sharing and talking honestly with others, I soon began creating mentorships and support groups where I could reach people on a deeper level, I began talking more in public about the things on my heart, and years later, thanks to those experiences, I was able to write this book. Now that I look back and see how God helped lead me toward those opportunities and gave me the confidence to think I could do it. I realize now my music was always meant to be just a small part of my overall purpose. As a result, I can totally own the overall work he's called me to do, which will last my entire life whether I'm in the spotlight or not.

You have that same overall purpose and space you were meant to fill—and a place you were meant to walk into and own. But sometimes the enemy will have us doubt our being. He'll even put people around you who will question your very existence. But God knows what we have inside and how it can come to fruition.

We all encounter examples of this kind of doubt toward who we are. For example, I remember walking onto a plane, and the flight attendant used a hand gesture for me to move toward the back of the plane. Not that there's a class that makes you any better, but I won't forget how hard it was for her to believe I was in first class. Granted, I had on a head wrap. I didn't look appropriate. My parents taught me better. However, my assigned seat was in first class. She asked to see my boarding pass, as if she didn't believe me, so I showed her. I didn't step out of character or get too bothered by her belief system because I knew where I was supposed to be. And while her judgment was (hopefully) only based on my relaxed look that day, we all receive similar judgments based on how we "appear" to be—and are told we are too shy or too bold to take on a role, or we have the wrong type of background, or we can't learn that skill, or that it's even crazy to try because that dream is just too big for us and it will hurt too much to fail.

When I think about those kinds of doubts and what they can do to us, I often think of the Israelites in Canaan. How much faster would they have gotten to the promised land—which God had already told them was theirs to take—if they'd just owned what was true about themselves as God's chosen people? When the twelve spies came back from Canaan, ten of them went around camp with the purpose of bringing everyone down, making the people believe they were nothing but tiny grasshoppers who couldn't do anything but wait to be crushed by the giants who were currently living in the land. Only Joshua and Caleb looked at what was possible, because they decided to look beyond appearances and remember what they had been promised ever since they'd left Egypt, and what God could do through them if they let him. And guess which men were the only ones who got to see the promised land—and help take it over—forty years later?

Maybe you're in a certain place and people can't believe you've come this far. Don't doubt yourself and don't think you don't deserve to be there. Have peace in knowing you are right where you should be and not everyone will like it. And while the spiritual attacks on us aren't always clear or obvious, they can be handled by remembering the "seat" we've been assigned to take, and walking toward it with confidence, knowing it's just waiting for us to claim it because it's already ours.

So stay strong and hold tight to where you belong. Look the enemy in the face and stand your ground. You have the right to be where God has placed you and Satan doesn't have the authority to boot you out or take away your opportunities. Tell yourself, "I'm supposed to be here." Nothing can move you unless you let it.

**prayer**

*Father, help me to see that I am supposed to be here. Show me how to own the gifts you have given me, and the space that I am in. I ask that you superimpose your confidence onto me and restore me to the place you've always intended for me to live inside. I thank you for this new place you've brought me to. This place is one of property value, lucrativeness, and it is a place that flows with milk and honey. Please don't let me see myself as a grasshopper. Help me see myself as you see me. You obviously think that I am big in heart, big in strength, and big in trust. Though this may be a place that you are still preparing me for, that may be occupied, I trust that you are giving me everything I need to securely rest, and operate, in this place. Amen.*

_scriptures to consider

They spread among the Israelites a bad report about the land they had explored. They said, "The land we explored devours those living in it. All the people we saw there are of great size. We saw the Nephilim there (the descendants of Anak come from the Nephilim). We seemed like grasshoppers in our own eyes, and we looked the same to them."

NUMBERS 13:32–33

Joshua son of Nun and Caleb son of Jephunneh, who were among those who had explored the land, tore their clothes and said to the entire Israelite assembly, "The land we passed through and explored is exceedingly good. If the Lord is pleased with us, he will lead us into that land, a land flowing with milk and honey, and will give it to us. . . . Their protection is gone, but the Lord is with us. Do not be afraid of them."

NUMBERS 14:6–9

# CHAPTER 26

# Say Less

Very often, I've found I have a lot to say. And talking too much is something I am very mindful of, because there have been people I've said I never wanted to be like simply because of how much *they* say. Recently, I even asked my friend Courtney, "Do I talk too much?" I then spoke with my parents about my talking habit while writing this chapter and my grandfather jokingly added, with a hint of seriousness, "My sweet grandbaby just talks so much!" I laughed, but it stuck with me! From that moment forward, I started gathering Scripture and truths about the tongue and about wisdom with our words, because it's important that our words carry lasting power, not just float on the wind and out of people's ears. And I've gathered that with the vision, dream, anointing, responsibility, and more that we all have, we have a calling to be mindful with our words.

In the past, I would sometimes say things I didn't mean or I felt the need to make conversation because it was so silent around me. It was like I couldn't control the things falling out of my mouth. It would then be hard for me to own things I said out of emotion, or easy to respond with the same venom I had received. Unacceptable! And some-times as I developed new relationships, they'd think I didn't know certain things. In response, I would always verbalize what I knew. I was ready to inform them of so much when I felt it was necessary to prove my intelligence, and over-whelm them with facts in the process. Or I would just share and share things about myself, even if we weren't in a tight relationship where that level of trust was earned. Eventually, I changed what I shared and when, and I allowed people to think what they wanted. I had to convince myself not to say everything but to instead leave some back for myself, because as we talked about before, if you release everything to the public, what will you have for yourself? And in the process, I learned that if I'm less busy trying to find words, I have more room to observe. Observing is a way to learn, dis-cern, and know how to proceed. I laughed at this, because this was something my grandmother would've told me. I remember my nanna often saying, "Too much! Too much!" Or my father telling me, "Sometimes the smartest answer to give is 'I don't know.'" Once I learned that, *I don't know* saved me from so much trouble. *I don't know* has also gotten my name out of drama, removed certain people from my life who didn't have to be there, and challenged me to own a freedom from any guilt I felt after leaving a room and not saying very much. I had to remind myself it is totally fine to not have the answer to everything. Sadly, I have noticed that many young women, because they have become so informationally informed, forget listening can sometimes give you more answers than knowledge will. Listening is an important skill to practice that benefits any relationship you will ever have. (And if you desire marriage, you'll especially have to do more of that in the covenant.) Saying less also shows a sign of selflessness.

But don't get me wrong; sometimes the answers we need are revealed when we release what is brewing inside us. So I'm not telling you to always sit there and be quiet, because speaking up for yourself and others or saying things that need to be said are important. We're not called to sit in the corner! It's more about being mindful and identifying when you (and others) have gotten tired of hearing your own voice. Because when people know your words carry meaning, instead of just being words, they'll know what you are saying carries weight and they will listen.

That balance of knowing when to speak is likely why the Bible often talks about our words alongside the idea of wisdom. While studying, I read Ecclesiastes 10:12–14, which says, "Words from the mouth of the wise are gracious, but fools are consumed by their own lips. At the beginning their words are folly; at the end they are wicked madness—and fools multiply words." And Ecclesiastes 5:3 says, "Many words mark the speech of a fool." While transparency and open sharing may be refreshing to some, transparency paired with wisdom can be restoring for many. So I took this healthy challenge to prepare to be a better/wiser woman, daughter, friend, sister, to-be wife, and someday mother: I will be a better listener, and not ready to say *everything*. I will not be like a "dripping faucet" to those I'm in covenant with. I will not run my family and friends away because of my mouth. And trust me, this journey takes time. Even though I've been working on this challenge for a while, I've been listening to myself talk this week, and there are still moments where my mouth is leaking words!

Remember those posters in elementary school that read "Silence is golden"? If we're always busy talking, how will we learn about those around us, or keep ourselves from getting into trouble? Can the talkative observe their surroundings? "Even fools are thought wise if they keep silent, and discerning if they hold their tongues" (Proverbs 17:28). What words have you released you won't get back? Practice this godly challenge with me! Become wiser!

_____prayer

*Lord, help me to follow through with your wise teachings even when it comes to how much I give from my lips. Help me to be slow to speak. Father, I need your supernatural help, and confidence, to walk away, and so that I do not feel the need to win based on what I speak. Keep me out of trouble and remind me that my strength is my control of the tongue. Help me to be so secure within myself that I don't have to prove to others who I am inside. Cleanse my heart so that nothing harmful seeps out through my lips, and purify my thoughts so that what naturally comes out is like heaven. Amen.*

_____scriptures to consider

Too much talk leads to sin. Be sensible and keep your mouth shut.

**PROVERBS 10:19 (NLT)**

Those who guard their mouths and their tongues keep themselves from calamity.

**PROVERBS 21:23**

# Remind Yourself

Since we're working on becoming our truest and best selves, let's take a moment to consider the character we've built so far.

Look back at the spiritual journey and encounters you've had with God over the last weeks or months. How have you seen your relationship with him grow? How have you seen yourself grow? And how has your approach to friendships, romance, and bettering yourself changed? Look at what really has happened, as well as how you'd like to keep changing. Correct what you did wrong, but also acknowledge what you did right.

Sometimes we have people to celebrate us in these journeys, and it's important to recognize and appreciate that feedback. But it's even more meaningful to remind *yourself* of your accomplishments so far, especially when people seem to forget. Remind yourself that your good heart and good intentions have to do with being secure within yourself. I've had to learn to speak words of affirmation, assuring myself with God's promises. You don't have to wait on someone else to validate who you are! Sometimes finding validation within yourself comes with reflection. There's always an answer deeper inside. This is where solitude is beneficial for us. So remember who you truly are, instead of listening to what other people think about you or tell you about yourself—unless they are your trusted counsel or village. Take precious moments alone to reflect and recharge, which are necessary so you can love who you are, and appreciate/acknowledge your progress toward owning every part of yourself.

# CHAPTER 27

# The Drains and the Fountains

**M**aybe leadership skills and a sense of purpose came with your makeup. Maybe you often find yourself being a counselor to many, but not always having the answers for yourself. For a while, I surrounded myself with people who always needed me—probably because I like pouring myself into others. And I've realized while looking at others around me, many powerful women gravitate toward that kind of needy person as well. I call these needy people drains, because even when you keep pouring the water, they never seem to get full and hold on to the gift.

Very often, I got the drains' issues confused with a problem on my end, because it was like the person was often stopped up, just not getting what I was trying to give.

So I worked harder, tried to explain in different ways, and gave more and more of my time and effort so they could start flowing on their own. But the reality is, these relationships couldn't digest the goodness that God had given me and I was sharing because their hearts and minds just weren't ready to hold the knowledge. As a result, because the content was passing right through even though the person looked like they were taking in water, I would sometimes mistake the drain for the promise of a fountain.

The fountain always has fresh content. It's like a spring—the water that goes in remains and is constantly flowing up and out, refining itself in the process. That's because Jesus is the well that never runs dry. Our relationships should reflect this part of his character—taking in the water he gives us, then using it to fill up those around us with its clean and refreshing power.

However, humans aren't perfect fountains like Jesus was—in order for us to function properly, we need to make sure our fountain stays in working order, and new water is poured into us when the pool starts to run dry. So if we are always pouring and we don't have a pourer around us, how do we expect to be filled? That's where the drains come back into the picture. If you're mainly surrounding yourself with people you've been giving almost every drop to, and there is honestly nothing coming of your work, you might have to pull back your flow and consider where your water is better spent. Then go and find yourself some strong water sources who can fill you back up. Because the truth is, you can't help everyone—it's up to others to want to change after seeing what you have. And sometimes it might take multiple fountains for the drain to see they can become something watertight and solid! Or even meeting the ultimate well himself.

Once I started focusing my water on the people God was placing in my life—instead of people who were clearly only there to take from me—I saw my efforts grow and the kingdom benefit. And I had more to draw from and give as well.

_____**prayer**

*Father, please help me make good decisions when it comes to who I allow into my life, especially when it comes to helping others on their journeys. I ask that you give me the wisdom to be selective with the people I take on so I can see who is ready for me to pour into and who is only there to take. And give me the strength to sustain those fountain relationships even when they get hard. I give you my life and everything that is in it. I understand that whatever I have is from you. So Father, lead and guide on what is to be given and who it is to be given to. I ask that you help me manage the relationships in my life so I am not overextending or overstepping boundaries in a way that could cause an aftermath of dread and defeat. I ask that you guide me on what should be kept between you and me, and direct me when it's time to release my spiritual waters to those around me. I need filling as well, so please walk alongside me* while I work through the changes you're having me to make in myself, and show me the fountains I can go to when needed. I give you this part of my life. Allow me to communicate effectively and love freely. May others experience heaven when they connect with me. In Jesus' name, I pray. Amen.

_____scriptures to consider

"Whoever believes in me, as Scripture has said, rivers of living water will flow from within them."

**JOHN 7:38**

Blessed are those who hunger and thirst for righteousness, for they will be filled.

**MATTHEW 5:6**

# CHAPTER 28

# Closure

Unfortunately, some things just won't work the way we hoped they would. The challenge is to get to a place where you're not always searching for closure, and instead are more concerned with simply ending it when the time comes.

Don't give curiosity the opportunity to draw you back into a place that isn't ordained by God. For a long time, I had a hard time letting things go without understanding exactly what had happened in a relationship or business deal, or without receiving an explanation that made sense to me. However, I've learned when God says, "That ain't it," that should be enough. Moving away from things that were actually harming me without fully realizing it has been hard, but in many circumstances it's led to some of my best decisions. For instance, I noticed friends I had in high school and in college distanced themselves when I decided to follow a path of discretion while they took on the YOLO motto. I would often feel alone. They'd leave me out. I didn't get invited to everything. I was either treated like the young buck or the "too saved one." My truth was that I wasn't perfect, and I wasn't attempting to give off "too saved" vibes, but I also wasn't going to denounce my salvation so I could have "a good time"; I was trained to remember I had more at stake, and that there was a tomorrow my unborn children would have to see. I'll stop there, because that's another book within itself. But I didn't have closure with those relationships. I wanted to know why they blocked me without having a conversation. I began saying I had nothing left for them, when the truth was, I was hurt and disappointed at how easy it had been for them to release me.

Now, I'm not at all implying I was the rough rider from heaven, but I did try and do my part. Unfortunately, I didn't get closure with them, so I had to close it on my own. What does that look like? It looks like accepting the apology you may never get from them. My old friends began coming around as we got older, and during that time I was convicted and guided to understand what I hadn't been able to grasp before—that it was easier to ignore me and the life I'd chosen than face the decisions they were making. And through the Lord's nudging, I began to feel the need to let go of what happened when we were yet growing and trying to figure ourselves out. And like fall has to come around every year, this is a process that occurs seasonally in our lives. We have to shed the things we've been holding on to in order to grow in the future.

Another experience I had of closing the door with God's help was when my nanna passed in April 2020. I still can't believe she's gone. The Lord gave me such peace and comfort when it all happened. But as the days went on, I'd have it in my mind to go and see her. It seemed like my grief was getting worse. One day I just started asking while in a room alone, "Why didn't you let me say bye to her?" I even asked, "Why didn't you give me a chance to know if she was being treated well while in the hospital?" I became angry with the Lord. There was something else rising in me, making me bold enough to verbalize my concerns. It started in my mind and went to a different kind of audacity. My mother said to me, "Be angry but sin not . . ." Whatever was rising in me became subject to God, and as I felt his presence, I began crying even harder. The Lord had me remember the comfort and answers he had given me earlier on this journey. I began realizing our lives aren't truly ours; they belong to the Lord. My nanna would have pulled me all the way together and said, "Don't question God and his doing about MY life." He brought me memories of what she'd say about this life and how she wasn't anxious to stay long, but most of all, he reminded me of how my nanna lived in public and behind closed doors. There wasn't a difference. She loved the Lord and she lived for him.

Around this time, a long-time friend called and said that they'd had a dream where I was crying hysterically about the loss of my grandmother, and wanted to tell me the Lord would give me comfort and closure concerning this. They even mentioned prayers my grandmother had talked to me about before, but all together their call was proof the Lord had sent me another reminder that all was well. A day after this call, I began a habit of sitting on my back deck, just to enjoy the weather and pray. I started seeing butterflies in my backyard and saw them in the front of my home literally every day. Call me weird if you'd like, but my grandmother loved butterflies. I'd see butterflies that were almost as big as a bird. They were additional clear signs of the Lord making sure I knew that her legacy, and lessons, will always be with me. The butterflies didn't make me sad, like they might have before; they made me smile. I strongly believe the Lord gives us signs, and speaks to us, through nature. Especially after I read about butterflies and their meaning and learned they represent resurrection.

Through all these messages, it was like the Lord was completing a work in me. Growing me up and helping me take ownership of what I'd learned from my journey with him as well as embrace the lessons from my grandmother. He reminded me what it meant to be a believer, and of the Scripture 2 Corinthians 5:8: "We are confident, I say, and would prefer to be away from the body and at home with the Lord." This was my nanna's conversation. As believers, we have a different, higher type of closure to guide us through life. And sometimes our closure is found in the revealed mysteries that are given to us while walking with the Lord.

Maybe you've been praying about an opportunity, relationship, a home purchase, a new job, or another thing on your mind. Just because it doesn't go through, that doesn't mean something else that is meant to be isn't around the corner. There's also the possibility some things are "open ended." Or maybe like me, you're struggling with closure over a loss that feels impossible to overcome. Not having an answer to everything is simply part of life, and nothing in this life is forever. Trust God's timing and way of doing things. Because if we stay stuck in the questions, we'll never get the real answers we need.

_____prayer

*Father, thank you for my best days! Remind me of the ways I can move forward and progress, and take away the desire to look back at the things that no longer benefit me. Lord, I thank you for changing my spiritual taste buds and showing me better, more nourishing food. I acknowledge that when I've taken things into my own hands, I've sort of screwed things up. I am not in denial; I am in truth. I'll admit that sometimes I hold on to things because I'm not sure if there's something better. But God, I know you'd only want the best for me. So, help me to take it one step at a time so that I am trusting you instead of holding on to questions that don't truly need answers. Amen.*

"Heaven and earth will pass away, but my words will never pass away."

**LUKE 21:33**

Even birds and animals have much they could teach you; ask the creatures of earth and sea for their wisdom. All of them know that the Lord's hand made them. It is God who directs the lives of his creatures; everyone's life is in his power.

**JOB 12:7–10 (GNT)**

# CHAPTER 29

# People Problems

We've been putting in the work of accepting and owning who we are—be it our big personality or dress size, our bold vision and drive, our beauty of character, or even a physical feature we now like staring at in the mirror. But that's only part of the journey. In addition to evaluating how we deal with ourselves, we also have to own and accept how we deal with others.

I remember being so annoyed with people that it began showing in my disposition. I once started a conversation with God by saying people were just annoying, and I preferred to be by myself. The Lord gave me the Scripture 2 Timothy 1:7 from the Living Bible: "For the Holy Spirit, God's gift, does not want you to be afraid of people, but to be wise and strong, and to love them and enjoy being with them." I responded, "I'm not *afraid* of them . . ." And the Lord responded to me with, "But I said, I want you to *enjoy being with them*. So hush!"

This experience with God helped me realize that a part of loving him is loving his people. Even the annoying ones. It also allowed me to see a truth about myself, and that truth was I had a hint of reservation when it came to dealing with others. Due to previous experiences, I wanted to avoid anyone who looked similar to a person I'd dealt with before. I was afraid of being judged, and I didn't want to deal with constant confrontation, or subtle comments, or simply sensing their thoughts about me. And I definitely didn't want to revisit problems or experiences I thought I had already gotten over with someone else. I was to a place where I was totally fine with simply being alone and not having to deal with people. However, from what I understand, God's Word assures us I won't be the only person who will make it into heaven. Hence, there will be others to love and fellowship with. So how do I expect to fit in with God's heavenly plans if I don't know how to deal with his people? That doesn't mean I have to agree with everything they do, and that doesn't mean they have to agree with everything I do, but it does mean I need to find some good in the encounters with people who challenge me and my patience.

I've had to elevate my way of thinking so that I'm able to exist in a world with people. One way of doing that has been simply understanding we all come from different villages. We come into situations with the cultures of our parents' homes as well as the cultures we've adapted for our own homes (even if it's not a physical home yet), the ways we communicate within those homes, as well as the insecurities we have, the traditions we carry, our learned ways of thinking, and so much more. And a lot of those things are behaviors and mindsets we're not even totally aware of all the time. That's a lot to consider when dealing with people, and that's a lot people have to consider when dealing with me! As a result, we oftentimes can misinterpret each other and will forever be annoyed by someone who may mean no harm, all due to a simple matter of colliding cultures. As an example, for one person, loud music may be a natural part of every celebration. For another person, playing classical music in the background may be their go-to party playlist. These languages of expression can then be misunderstood as aggression or as someone thinking they're better than others, when it may not be that at all. And if the two sides never talk or engage with each other—civilly—then those misunderstandings just get worse over time.

I've had to learn to ignore some annoying behaviors I am not able to fully understand in the moment because I grew up in a different type of world. I've also learned that connecting with people with the intention of breaking down some of those barriers between worlds is a beautiful way of globalizing ourselves, correcting damaging behaviors or assumptions, sharpening ourselves through accountability, as well as discovering other ways of living, creating a new safe space we can both inhabit, and so on. And in practicing that in my life, I've changed how I deal with (and react to) the people I meet briefly, and the ones I choose to deal with on a deeper level long term.

I had to learn this the hard way. I come from a family who is generous. We give what we can, when we can, and if we can give more, we'll absolutely do it. So it was a shock when I discovered that with some people, as long as you give it, they will gladly take it. For instance, if some new friends and I went out to eat and I paid, I didn't ask for the money back. But when it was their turn to pay, oh honey-chile, they were expecting every dime back. It could be the smallest amount. I shouldn't have faulted them for this, but I was used to being with my family, and close friends, fighting over a bill when it was time to pay. We were always ready to take care of each other because it was our language of love toward each other. However, over time, my new friends' behavior continued to bother me more and more, until I learned their reaction was simply because their family's approach was different. I've had to consider this information in multiple relationships. It's not fair to expect that just because you have something and are able to give it, someone who simply does not have it needs to respond in kind. It's like asking for orange juice from an apple—it doesn't produce it! I also now pay attention to people who simply didn't WANT to give it. The difference has helped me choose who is a real friend. When we look at where we've been and what we repeat, it helps us evaluate the new people we meet; or if someone presents us with a new experience, we can learn from that relationship and apply it to the next. Awkwardness in times of tested loyalty is to be noticed and considered.

And only you can control how you react and the decisions you make. My father often told me, "If someone can get you to act out of character, or without control of your emotions, they have control over you, and no one should have control over you. You should have control of yourself." Plus, God called us to be authoritative creatures. He doesn't want us to lose control. And part of controlling yourself is remembering it goes both ways: you can't control other people's thoughts and actions any more than they should control yours. No one belongs to you or has to follow your choices. So don't put your expectations or experiences on others. Even those connected to your friends and significant others—you may have to share them with people who rub you the wrong way, or people who will always be hard for you to understand. But some people come into your life with a purpose outside of you. In those cases, you just have to step aside, be the best version of you, and let it be. As big as your journey may feel, there's always something bigger going on with God.

And even if your character is good and you're growing in your awareness, you'll have bad moments in your interactions with people. At the same time, though you may be a great person at heart, you may also be a part of someone else's expired season—an interaction that is more about their ultimate journey than yours.

What has kept me in a peaceful place is allowing difficult people to be who they are and trying to accept our differences, unless I am close enough to sharpen them if there is a genuine issue we need to explore. Otherwise, I own and mind my business.

_____**prayer**

*Father, help me to find joy in my interactions! Help me to love without fear. Direct me in ways to grow and be wise, to ignore the annoyances and address the actual issues. Help me to decide when I should walk away, and when I should stay. Don't allow me to milk a bad day, dwelling on it to the point I leave a connection that may benefit me for a lifetime. Give me the perseverance to dig deeper and love harder. Have me operate with the insight you've promised me. Help me identify the spirit in which others operate, and give me the strength to shut any negativity down immediately. I accept the fact no one belongs to me. I release to you the people I hold dear to my heart who need help I cannot give. I accept your healthy balance when it comes to relationships—those who are in my life for a moment and those I need to grow with. I make the commitment before you to let people live their lives so that I can be free to live mine. I trust that this is a new journey you're allowing me to experience.*

We love because he first loved us. Whoever claims to love God yet hates a brother or sister is a liar. For whoever does not love their brother and sister, whom they have seen, cannot love God, whom they have not seen. And he has given us this command: Anyone who loves God must also love their brother and sister.

1 JOHN 4:19–21

# Lower Your Expectations

There's such a thing as having different relationship levels with different people. And it's sometimes the best way to go. You have some friends who are just fun to be with, but maybe you don't share too many secrets with them. You have some people in your circle who are socially awkward, but you catch a vibe when it's only you and them. Or maybe there's someone in a totally different state, and the only thing that makes the difference is the distance. I have a friend who makes me laugh hysterically when she doesn't even mean to. I know if I call her, she'll come through for me, keep my secrets, and pray for me.

Knowing how to navigate relationships is so important because sometimes God will use people to give us answers or lessons, or to act as mirrors. Relationships are also a part of the abundance in life that God promises us. Jonathan and David were covenant brothers who faced a lot of challenges to their relationship, yet they grew despite of—and sometimes because of—those challenges. So, are there friendships we can grow even when it seems like things are hard around the relationship? I've also had to ask myself, "Am I always at odds with a certain person?" And if so, is the reason something worth losing the person over? I never want to fall out with a potential solution to my problem. As a result, I've begun changing my expectations and not expecting people to give what I give them. I've also begun forgiving and not waiting for an apology from certain people. I make it a priority to communicate but to not expect the other person to always agree with what *I* feel is right. And my relationships have grown in their own ways as a result.

So cultivate your friendships and be open to different types of relationships. Each person in our lives can bless us in unique and special ways.

# CHAPTER 30

# Putting Down the Weight of Guilt and Picking Up the Weight of Glory

While working on my weight, I learned the difference between muscle weight and fat weight. Muscle weight in denser and takes up less space. It improves bones and helps burn calories, as well as assists us to live longer. While fat weight increases the risks of heart disease, high blood pressure, strokes, and more. The unhealthy weight that puts us more at risk is what the weight of guilt will also do in our lives. Knowing the difference between the life-giving weight of glory and the life-stealing weight of guilt is so necessary to help us pull it together and walk securely in our lives and purposes. In my life, the weight of guilt caused me to question every part of my being. Hence, I was unable to live in peace. The weight of guilt caused me to question which people I could actually trust. This weight became so big and heavy, it didn't fit into my happy place. It didn't allow me to sit and look pretty. It didn't allow a graceful poise. This weight caused me to question my beauty. Even when I reached a happy place, guilt made me feel like I was wrong for being there.

And this battle with guilt started to change my interactions. I'd often feel guilty for correcting someone, even in the kindest way, for mishandling me. Then after I went through a time of not speaking up for myself, I shifted gears to being vocal and not just taking *anything* people had to offer or suggest. As a result, I often felt like a problem, and that guilt added to all the other guilty feelings piling up inside. I even noticed that because of my way of adapting to life—trying to control everything because I thought I had to—I attracted manipulative people who only brought me down and added to my uneasiness with myself and how I should act. At this point, it was no one's fault but mine, because I was a woman of faith not using the information God had given me in his Word. I was fighting the fight, but I hadn't gone deep enough to remember that the adversary isn't just someone who walks around with a red tail and horns—he is "the accuser of our brothers and sisters" (Revelation 12:10). The adversary often works through people, who let him. It's part of his agenda to make us feel like our very being is wrong. He wants us uncertain of where we should stand, and he tears down our confidence and confuses us about who we are. He accuses us of things that we didn't really do, or paralyzes us for sticking up for ourselves. He suggests we question our decisions, including the ones that are based around godly thinking. And the guilt, confusion, and feeling ineffective and wrong provide a way for the seeds he plants to get a grip inside us.

I remember someone telling me that having an honest conversation with me while I was attempting to gain clarity on an issue was disheartening for them. Why? Why would my getting clarity be a heartbreak for you? I realized it was because they weren't used to me asking questions. They didn't want me to become privy to their game. I learned in this experience that they were more concerned I would see their true colors than they were actually disturbed by something I said. And once I had that breakthrough, a lot of the guilt around how I appropriately handled myself went away. I didn't feel bad about questioning the things that had to be questioned, and I saw I could trust the people who passed the test and actually had my back. I no longer had to feel guilty about my decisions, as long as I was using grace and insight. And I could accept being in my happy place because I knew I'd gotten there by using God's words and wisdom instead of my weighed-down and confused mindset.

Don't forget to own who you are in this battle. The enemy wants us blind to the truth. You are a part of the gospel, and don't let anyone make you feel like you're wrong for being big in your faith, with your glory, and with your truth. Your being clear and aware of what's happening around you is part of the Master's plan. God wouldn't dare leave you without a clue and have you to feel wrong about figuring it out. When we play trivia games, we get excited when we figure out the answer, right? So get excited about figuring out the strategy of your opponent, knowing how to fight the fight to successfully win. And be confident in the fact you have authority over him and the tactics he uses against you. And if you're following God's guidance, you're not guilty! You've been acquitted. Christ paid the price for you to fly high effortlessly and straight like an eagle. May your weightless journey always remind you of the glory that is on your life. Be free and be blameless.

_____**prayer**

*Father, don't allow me to let people bully me through manipulation, be it professionally, in a mentoring relationship, within a friendship, or anything else. Help me operate with the insight you promised me as your heir. Help me identify the spirit by which people operate so I can discern if they come to make me feel guilty or if they come to offer me correction. Give me the strength to shut the negative thoughts down immediately. And give me the wisdom to act according to your Word so I have no reason to feel guilty about myself and my actions. Remind me of your teachings every day. In Jesus's name, amen.*

*Big, Bold, and Beautiful*

In their case the god of this world has blinded the minds of the unbelievers, to keep them from seeing the light of the gospel of the glory of Christ, who is the image of God.

2 CORINTHIANS 4:4 (ESV)

Let us draw near to God with a sincere heart and with the full assurance that faith brings, having our hearts sprinkled to cleanse us from a guilty conscience and having our bodies washed with pure water.

HEBREWS 10:22

# CHAPTER 31

# Fearless and Unbothered

While being in quarantine during Covid-19, I wondered if I would be okay financially since work was slow during this time. I began having conversations with the Lord and I told him, "I have my emergency fund, but how long will this go on?" After consulting with the Lord, there was an immediate peace that overcame me. I wasn't worried. I slept even better that evening. A couple of days later, out of nowhere, my other streams of income increased. While I was worried about the aftermath of the quarantine, what settled my spirit was this God-given peace. Because when we have conversations with heaven, and are true to the women God called us to become, we receive a different kind of understanding. The Word says in Mark 4:11 that he'll give us the mystery of the kingdom of God. You and I are a part of that mystery.

When I'm tuned in with God, I have an understanding that allows me to move differently. This understanding lets me walk with no fear. God said that we'd be satisfied and would have plenty in the time of famine. I come from royalty, and I know who my Father is—dysfunction doesn't scare me. Chaos doesn't scare me. Confusion doesn't scare me. Pandemics don't scare me. Loud voices with anger and strength don't scare me. They shouldn't scare you either. This insight from heaven should cause us to be so still that our stillness scares *them*. Just like Queen Esther, we should be unmoved.

As women of God, we must understand how powerful we are. How the way is made easy when we are walking closely with him. This peace is guarding my heart and mind but also surpassing regular understanding. What people say is impossible, my faith helps me to understand that the impossible can be accomplished. My thought process is connected to the supernatural process. So regular human understanding doesn't stand a chance against this bigger way of "seeing," thinking, or believing.

When we own what makes us who we are and align with owning the path God has for us, God will give us a peace that cannot be moved or shaken. This peace allows us to sleep and dream again. But some of us haven't been able to dream big things because we've been interrupted by life's worries. The only way to overcome that is to remove any unnecessary distraction or seeds of doubt that are disturbing your peace. This could be people, circumstances, or even possessions we need to cast aside. Once I challenged myself to live this way, and started walking with this peace of mind; I began walking in authority. I wasn't easily moved. Some of my close friends would ask, "What's wrong with you?" or "Why aren't you responding like you used to?" It was because I had shifted myself away from the needless worries and past behaviors that were taking up my energy and focus, and I had officially allowed myself to fight for me and move on my behalf—to do the things that would increase my peace and make a difference in my life.

And if you struggle with taking on a mindset of peace, look to the people around you for examples. My mother is so graceful and peaceful. I've never really seen her spaz out. She's so still within her soul. While watching her just live and admiring her prayer life, I've learned that when you have peace, you don't do everything, or you may not even respond at all. Calmness is a superpower. The ability to not overreact, or take things personally, keeps your mind clear and your heart at peace.

_____prayer

*Father, please grow me up. Mature me. Show me how to grow in my relationship with you so that I am so steeled within my soul, when there's a storm I'm not worried or I don't move or react. Help me understand the power you truly have in your hands and that it is all in your control. I thank you for this peace you're offering me—that you are flowing into my mind and heart, changing the way I operate and the way I speak. I understand that with you on my side, you are always fighting for me. Thank you for being my comforter. Please remove any forms of confusion that may creep back in to steal my joy. Since you're the Prince of Peace, you know all about it. And since you are my creator, you know the areas where I need more peace. I look forward to receiving that gift.*

_____**scriptures to consider**

In times of disaster they will not wither; in days of famine they will enjoy plenty.

**PSALM 37:19**

I know what it is to be in need, and I know what it is to have plenty. I have learned the secret of being content in any and every situation, whether well fed or hungry, whether living in plenty or in want. I can do all this through him who gives me strength.

**PHILIPPIANS 4:12–13**

# Owning It All

We live in a culture where many things pull at our attention. So many people need our time. Distractions are assigned to knock us out of purpose. Emotions often cause us to make decisions that don't carry real quality. But in this space of becoming the woman God created me to be, and exploring who God made you to be, I've discovered that when we allow ourselves to be big in everything we do, to go forward with boldness and confidence, and to display our God-given beauty to the world, we achieve a deep and lasting peace.

And as you go forward, one of the secrets for this new phase in our lives is, "My decisions determine the quality of my peace."

Be very careful with who's in your space. Examine who you enter a relationship with—be it people you need to support you, people who seek support, or a man. Examine who they are, test them against what God whispers in your heart. And once you have the people you need to keep you on track, make that space you are building a location where you deal with what's going to actually benefit you and those around you, and not just what's at the forefront begging for your time. Then examine yourself—what you're holding on to, what you truly need, and what you are called to accomplish. By doing what you need to do, and staying true to what makes you the amazing woman you are inside, you are ensuring you're operating as a whole individual and pulling together all of the pieces of yourself, making you whole and functional again. Which sets you up to go on and help others on the same journey.

Lately, I've tried to put everything I've learned about myself into practice in order to own who I am supposed to be and find my peace with others and myself. I decided to have family and friends who are safe filters and voices of reason. If the room is quiet, I'm not making it my job to fill the room with noise or to spark deep conversations with people I'm not sure of yet. I am making the decision to observe and not ignore what I discern. I have been praying with a heart of repentance and removing the weight of guilt from my heart. I ask questions for clarity from a place of confidence and understanding. And before responding, I pause and ask myself, "Will this feeling pass, or is there more to it I need to take note of and act on?" I've promised myself to be fair but to keep peace with myself and others.

As we grow and find who we are, it's important to make sure our past issues don't come back to undo our future. Owning it is a lifelong process of refining yourself and moving closer to your godly, royal form. *Royal* is associated with the idea of being superior, of kingly ancestry, being suitable for a role, a person of royal blood, and established. Royalty doesn't fit in all places. Some may view royalty to be odd or too different. But just because they can't fathom it, or don't understand it, doesn't mean that it has to change or is wrong. So don't change this great part of you. Stay in tune to our God, who speaks and who will reveal a strategy for our lives that will lead us where we need to go.

The peace and quiet confidence I have discovered to be the one and only, big and bold Kierra Sheard-Kelly in this process is everything. I pray you receive the same life-changing and life-giving confidence in yourself, and inner peace with your soul as well. Own it. Someone once said, "Think big, dream big, believe big, and the results will be big." We serve a big God and he is our Father. Therefore, there is nothing small about us. Embrace your big. Be bold about it and know that God's beauty and glory rests on you.

ACKNOWLEDGMENTS

I want to acknowledge every person who is responsible for this great opportunity and dream. I am so blessed to say that I have had the chance to be an author in this lifetime. Thank you, Zondervan, for giving me a chance, along with the other representatives who helped me carry this out: Jacque Alberta, Jessica Westra, Sara Merritt, and my Maya.

Head over to these sites for more Kierra Sheard-Kelly content, including video posts, Katching Kierra episodes, and motivational content, as well as information on her music and upcoming tours.

 @kierrasheard

 @kierrasheard

 KierraSheardVEVO

@kierrasheard

www.iamkierrasheard.com

K ierra Sheard-Kelly is a singer, songwriter, actress, and activist from Detroit, Michigan, who looks to express herself and inspire others in everything she does. Part of the next generation of the legendary gospel group the Clark Sisters, Kierra began her solo career in 2004, most recently releasing the album *KIERRA*, which includes a collaboration with Missy Elliot. She's also created her own clothing line entitled Eleven60, is completing her master's degree in clinical psychology, and works with organizations dedicated to youth and female empowerment.